CONSUMER TACTICS MANUAL

Books by John Dorfman

CONSUMER TACTICS MANUAL *1980*

WELL-BEING: AN INTRODUCTION TO HEALTH *1980*

A CONSUMER'S ARSENAL *1976*

CONSUMER SURVIVAL KIT *1975*

CONSUMER TACTICS MANUAL

How to Get Action on Your Complaints

JOHN DORFMAN

Atheneum New York 1980

Library of Congress Cataloging in Publication Data

Dorfman, John.
Consumer tactics manual.

1. Consumer protection—United States.
I. Title.
HC110.C63D67 1980 381'.33 80-65987
ISBN 0-689-11105-3
ISBN 0-689-11115-0 (pbk.)

Published simultaneously in Canada by McClelland and Stewart Ltd.
Manufactured by American Book–Stratford Press,
Saddle Brook, New Jersey
Designed by Mary Cregan
First Edition

To MICHAEL, *again*

Contents

TWO—How to Fight Back, From A to Z

Preface

In 1975, my first book was published. Called *Consumer Survival Kit,* and based on the television series of the same name, it was a guide to buying wisely. The publisher sent me on a publicity tour, and I appeared on a number of telephone call-in shows. I was amazed and interested to discover that close to 90 percent of the questions weren't concerned with how to buy things wisely. They were concerned with what to do when you've *already* bought something, and it's turned out to be unsatisfactory. My second book, *A Consumer's Arsenal* (1976), dealt with this common concern. What do you do when you've purchased something and it's no good? How do you get action on your complaints?

I thought many times about revising *A Consumer's Arsenal,* updating it, reorganizing it. In 1980, the time seemed ripe. Congress, in a justifiable effort to eliminate excessive regulation and red tape, was trampling heavily on the toes of federal regulatory agencies. Unfortunately, the line between unnecessary and necessary regulation was getting blurred, and many politicians were beginning to tilt against all regulation, including that needed to protect consumers. At such a time, it seemed to me particularly important that consumers be aware of their rights and avenues of recourse.

In 1980, the U.S. Office of Consumer Affairs was making a policy shift of its own. It was trying to get out of the business of processing consumer complaints. In the past, the OCA had often funneled complaints to the appropriate state or federal agencies. But OCA's administrators no longer felt this was the best use of that office's limited resources. That made it all the more important for consumers to know, themselves, where to turn for help.

OCA recognized this fact. In 1980 it published *Consumer's Resource Handbook,* a seventy-seven page booklet that is billed as a "what-to-do, where-to-go manual for resolving consumer problems." (Single copies are free from the Consumer Information Center, Dept. 532 G, Pueblo, CO 81009.) Much of the material in that handbook—as well as much material from my own research that is not found in the handbook—is found in *Consumer Tactics Manual.*

In writing *Consumer Tactics Manual,* I drew heavily on the contents of *A Consumer's Arsenal*—updated, of course. I have added expanded discussions of areas I felt needed further emphasis, such as discrimination, securities, and automobile repairs. And I've added new entries on taxes, Social Security, handicaps, and pensions. But, perhaps most important, I changed the organization. The book you are holding is really intended as a field manual. I want you to be able to use it—fast—to find a discussion of a particular consumer problem you're having. From that, I want you to be able to turn immediately to a discussion of the tactics or agencies that may be helpful to you. That's why this book is organized the way it is. Part I is an encyclopedia of problems, listed alphabetically. Part II is a discussion of how you can fight back, divided into twenty-six specific techniques. Most Part I entries refer you to a section or sections of Part II that may be appropriate for your particular complaint.

I hope you'll find this organization useful and the information in this book helpful. But if you want to get action on your complaints, nothing I can say in two hundred or so pages will be as important as your own attitude and persistence. If you've got a legitimate complaint, the most important advice can be summarized in four words: Stick to your guns.

Introduction

Professor David Klein, who teaches social science at Michigan State University, knows how to get action. Witness what he did when he arrived one night in Montreal to find that his hotel room, reserved long before, had been given to someone else.

"I will give you," he told the clerk, "three minutes to find me a room. After three minutes, I am going to undress in the lobby, put on my pajamas, and go to sleep on one of the sofas."

The professor never raised his voice. He got his room.

You *can* get some satisfaction. And it doesn't have to involve taking off your clothes.

In the transactions that fill much of your daily life, you have a choice. You can let things take their course, and periodically suffer the emotional and financial strain of being taken advantage of. Or you can hold out for satisfaction. Sometimes, a good deal of money's at stake. Sometimes not. Each person decides when to fight "for the principle of the thing," and when it's not worth the time and effort. I believe that insisting on being treated well and fairly is good for the soul. Not to mention the wallet.

This book won't make you a wise buyer of products and services.* It's intended to help you when—whether you were

* For that purpose, I recommend the Annual Buying Guide issue of *Consumer Reports* magazine; *Guide to Consumer Services,* by the editors of *Consumer Reports;* and *The New Consumer Survival Kit* by Richard George. A subscription to *Consumer Reports* magazine

wise or unwise—something's gone wrong. Your car's a lemon. Your new roof leaks. Your dishwasher drools on the floor. Your stereo speakers shout when they should whisper. The repairman who "fixed" your TV left it so that everyone on screen has red skin (except the Indians, who are purple).

Most of this book is devoted to situations in which you're the customer. But that's not the exclusive focus. We also discuss some problems you may encounter on the job: problems of discrimination by race, sex, or age; and problems you have with pollution. You may never buy anything from Amalgamated Widget, but if they fill your neighborhood with smoke, you've got some unfinished business to settle with them.

The book is arranged to make it as easy as possible for you to deal with any problem you've got. Part I of the book is a complaint encyclopedia. Most of the consumer problems you might have are listed alphabetically, along with cross-references. If you're having a problem with a correspondence school, for example, you'll find a cross-reference to vocational schools. Looking under vocational schools, you'll find some specific advice on dealing with some of the problems you might be having.

Part II of the book is called How to Fight Back—From A to Z. It describes twenty-six possible sources of help with any consumer problem or dispute. Some are techniques. Others are groups that are ready, willing, and often able to help you. The twenty-six strategies are arranged roughly in order of their power, from making a telephone call on up. The strategies form a complaint ladder with ten rungs. Here are the ten steps of the ladder, along with the corresponding key letters from the How to Fight Back section:

---

wouldn't hurt, either. If you're looking for investment advice, two of the best and most readable books are *A Random Walk down Wall Street,* by Burton Malkiel, and *The Only Investment Guide You'll Ever Need,* by Andrew Tobias.

The Complaint Ladder

Step 1	Telephone complaints (A)
Step 2	Complaint letters (B)
Step 3	Use of trade associations (C)
Step 4	Better Business Bureau (D)
Step 5	Local and state government complaint agencies (E and F)
Step 6	Federal complaint agencies (G, H, I, J, K, L, and M)
Step 7	Legal action (N, O, and P)
Step 8	Getting help from consumer groups (Q, R, and S)
Step 9	Getting help from the media (T and U)
Step 10	Advanced complaint tactics (V, W, X, Y, and Z)

Generally speaking, you should begin at the lower end of the ladder, working upward until you get satisfaction. Why not start with the most powerful applicable technique? First, because there's no point in making enemies needlessly. Businesses do make honest mistakes and should get a fair chance to rectify them. Second, by beginning at the bottom you are saving some tactics in reserve; if you go to court and lose, no one will care about your complaint to the Better Business Bureau; but if Amalgamated Widget fears you might go to court if they don't respond to your letters, the company may settle to avoid the expense of litigation. Third, the higher up the ladder you go, the more work is involved for you: It's more time consuming to deal with a state consumer agency than to write a complaint letter to the company. And fourth, by going up the complaint ladder, you will be creating a written record that government agencies or the courts (if you need them) can deal with—you'll improve your chances of winning if your dispute goes that far.

Of course, each complaint is different. You can't always start with Step 1 and work your way up. Feel free to apply common sense, to use your own judgment.

But many complaints do fall into familiar categories. Part I deals with most of the complaints you're most likely to have. So if something's griping you, start with the appropriate entry in Part I. It will give you some preliminary suggestions on coping with the problem, and will usually refer you to a specific entry in Part II for more details on who can help you, and how you can help yourself.

According to Washington legend, the late President John F. Kennedy liked to quote the saying, "Don't get mad, get even." You may want to get a bit of both. The important thing is that, if you put some effort into it, you can get satisfaction. It may cost you some time, and time is money, sure enough. But when you keep someone from taking unfair advantage of you, it does something for your self-esteem, your general sense of well-being. And it's likely not to be bad for your pocketbook either.

ONE

Complaint Encyclopedia

Advertising. The slightly misleading ad is the mosquito of the marketplace. The downright false ad is its wasp. If you've been bitten or stung, there are a number of places you can turn for help.

Where you turn depends on what you want. You may want fair treatment for yourself—e.g., your money back, or a product that lives up to the ad's claims. Or you may want to call a halt to the deception, to bring an end to the use of the ad. (In extreme cases, you might even aim to force the company into running corrective ads.)

There's no reason why you can't aim for both—fair treatment for yourself, and an end to the offending ads. But you should decide which is more important to you, and plan your strategy accordingly.

If you mainly want to get your money back, or to get the item you *thought* you had coming to you, then don't rush to complain to government agencies. Why not? Because that would force the company into a defensive posture, which might make it less likely for them to offer you a satisfactory settlement. What you should do is negotiate directly with the company, keeping in reserve the threat of involving government agencies. You may or may not need to bring this club out of the closet.

Case in point: A doctor on Long Island saw an ad for a cabinet that holds medical supplies. Pictured clearly in the ad was a cabinet with four drawers. Prominently displayed was a price. The doctor sent away for the cabinet, writing out a check for the amount shown. To his surprise, the cabinet that was delivered had only two drawers. He pulled out the ad and scanned it carefully. In tiny print at the bottom was a notice: The price quoted was for a two-drawer model; the model pictured could be had for a somewhat higher price. "The difference in price was peanuts to me," the doctor said. "But here I had spent my time ordering a cabinet that wouldn't hold all my supplies. I was fuming." He called the company and pointed out that the ad clearly gave the impression that a four-drawer model could be bought for the price shown in large type. The company, he said, had a choice. It could send the four-drawer model immediately, at no extra charge. Or it could take its chances on how legal officials would view the fine print in its ad. The company chose not to take that chance: The next day it sent out a delivery man who dropped off the larger cabinet and took the two-drawer one away.

The speed with which the company set things right in that instance may have been partly the result of the club-in-the-closet effect. Had the doctor complained to a government agency immediately, the company might have been less accommodating. It might have been pushed into a "we-didn't-do-anything-wrong" stance.

Let's say, though, that your main concern isn't for yourself; it's to get the company to drop what you consider an unfair ad. If that's the case, send a protest letter (see II-B) to the president of the company. Send photocopies, with a brief covering note, to some or all of the following:

1. The Federal Trade Commission
2. The National Advertising Division, Council of Better Business Bureaus
3. Your local Better Business Bureau
4. Your state consumer protection agency
5. The advertising manager of the newspaper, radio station, TV station, or magazine where you saw or heard the ad
6. The advertising agency that represents the company

A few brief comments on each of these possibilities are in order.

(1.) *The Federal Trade Commission* (see II-H) is specifically charged with investigating false or misleading advertising. Some people think that the FTC is only concerned with large, nationwide firms. That's not true. To come within the FTC's purview, a firm need only be large enough to "affect" interstate commerce.

Some people also think that the FTC stuffs complaints about misleading advertisements into a file drawer, and does nothing at all unless it receives many complaints about a particular firm. That happens to be, in my opinion, true. The FTC can't go after everyone, so it tends to go after those outfits on which it receives multiple complaints. Does this make it worthless to write the FTC? Not in my book; after all, how will it get a lot of complaints against a firm if it doesn't get yours?

When it does move against a firm, the FTC can trot out big guns, including the threat of a $10,000-a-day fine. Under the gun, many firms sign "consent orders" prohibiting future use of the disputed claims. The FTC can also require a firm to advertise that its previous claims were false or misleading. It can make a firm keep this up until the firm has spent a certain sum of money (usually figured as a percentage of the firm's previous advertising budget) on corrective ads. Or it can make the firm keep airing corrective ads until surveys show that a given percentage of the public understands the situation correctly.

Among the more celebrated firms involved in corrective advertising cases were Warner-Lambert, which had to advertise that Listerine didn't help prevent colds after all; and ITT Continental Baking, which had to proclaim that Profile bread contained fewer calories per slice than ordinary bread simply because it was sliced thinner.

(2) *The National Advertising Division, Council of Better Business Bureaus.* Call it NAD, if you like. This is a self-regulatory agency sponsored by the ad industry and the Council of Better Business Bureaus. It concerns itself solely with national advertising, and handles about two hundred complaints a year. When NAD was first set up, skeptics talked a lot about the fox guarding the chicken coop, and the like. In practice, NAD has often taken a tough stance against ads that could mislead consumers. For example, NAD got Hardee's Food Systems to stop using the term "charco-broiled," which implied (thought it did not state) that the food was broiled over charcoal. In fact, it was grilled on ceramic briquettes.

NAD's official powers are nil. It relies entirely on persuasion. But it can be quite persuasive, by arguing to the business community that if self-policing doesn't work, tougher government regulations are likely to follow.

The big beef against NAD has been that it takes too long to resolve complaints. In 1975, *The New York Times* reported that the average complaint took NAD six to nine months to process. At that pace, there's a good chance that an ad will have been dropped (in the natural course of advertising cycles) before NAD tells the offender to stop using it. Officials of NAD were conscious of this criticism and have been working to trim down complaint-handling time. Still, it's often around six months.

If you want to complain to NAD, write National Advertising Division, Council of Better Business Bureaus, 845 Third Ave., New York, N.Y. 10028.

(3) *Your local Better Business Bureau* (see II-D). Sure, they're business oriented, but in some communities BBBs can be quite effective, and a useful help to consumers. Your local BBB is specifically concerned with local advertising. They

won't ignore a complaint against Joe's Roofer just because it's a small outlet.

Complaining to the BBB can accomplish three things. First, the BBB may be able to help you get your money back, or your whatever-it-is repaired or replaced. Second, the BBB may persuade the offending business to drop the claim from its ads. Third, your complaint goes on file at the local BBB office. Businesses that exceed a threshold number of complaints, or that fail to respond to complaints, may have an unfavorable report given out to people who call the BBB to ask about a firm's reputation.

(4) *Your state consumer protection agency.* If an ad was fraudulent or distinctly misleading, these agencies are your best bet for getting corrective legal action. In some states, the consumer protection agency is within the state attorney general's office. In other states, it's separate. If it's separate in your state, send copies of your complaint to both.

A detailed rundown on the state agencies is found in II-F.

(5) *The advertising manager of the newspaper, radio station, TV station, or magazine where you saw or heard the ad.* Some of the media have established "advertising acceptability" departments to review complaints from the public and to screen out ads from undesirable businesses. If there's such a department, use it. If not, try to talk or write to the head of the advertising department.

(6) *The advertising agency that represents the company.* This is a long shot, but it can at times be effective. Not many consumers go to the trouble of finding out who writes the ads a big company uses. For that very reason, a complaint letter that finds its way to the person who wrote the ad can carry a surprising amount of weight.

You can often find out who the ad agency is by consulting the *Standard Dictionary of Advertisers* (National Register

Publishing Co., Skokie, Illinois), found in many libraries. (A companion volume, *Standard Dictionary of Advertising Agencies,* may also be helpful.) Then you address your letter along these lines: Account Executive, Universal Tomahawk, Sharp & Carp Advertising Agency.

No matter which of these six routes you use, it helps to provide as specific an account of the offending ad as you can. If the ad was in print, a photocopy should be provided if possible. For broadcast ads, do your best to be specific about the airing time and station. Also specify exactly what you found to be wrong about the ad. A sample:

> On August 11, between 8:30 and 9 A.M., I heard an ad on WZIZ radio for a product called the Miraculous Mower. The ad said the product "will trim your hedges, and can also be used for cutting your hair." When I purchased the product, I found it did little to my hedges but made quite a dent in my scalp. This advertisement is, in my opinion, misleading and deceptive. I have requested from Miraculous Mowers, Inc. a full refund, plus $30 for medical treatment. I am writing to you in hope that you can bring about an end to the use of the ad. A copy of my letter to Mr. Kenneth Malicious, president of Miraculous Mowers, is enclosed.

And now for a word about ingratitude. You'll recall that we've outlined two approaches, one for "getting yours" (write the company first), and the other for seeing that the advertiser "gets his" (complaining to third parties). If you have gotten yours, there's no reason to stop there unless you want to. Some people may call this biting the hand that just placated you. But if you're angry enough about the deception, you may feel justified in doing just that. Fiorello LaGuardia, the celebrated mayor of New York, is said to have remarked, "One thing that qualifies me for this job is my monumental ingratitude."

Age Discrimination. See Discrimination.

Air Conditioners. See Appliances and Appliance Repairs.

Airlines. The comedian Shelly Berman's main concern was that a plane might "come to a sudden stop—like against a mountain." Most airline complaints are considerably less dramatic than that. They tend to deal with ticket overcharges, bumping, delays, flight cancellations, and lost or damaged luggage.

It helps if you know what your rights are. Let's look at your rights in each of several common air travel snafus.

If you're overcharged for a ticket, you're entitled to the difference between what you paid and what you should have paid. Overcharges aren't unusual, given the baroque structure of airline fares.

If you're bumped from a flight for which you held a reservation, you're entitled to what's called "denied boarding compensation." The Civil Aeronautics Board (CAB) recently increased the amount of compensation you get. At a minimum, you're entitled to ride the next available plane *and* to get a full refund on the price of your ticket, up to a maximum of $200. However, if you're delayed more than two hours in reaching your destination city, you're entitled to additional compensation—*twice* the value of your ticket, up to a maximum of $400. The aim is to discourage bumping; if the side effect is to make you feel better about having been bumped, so much the better. A couple of details: The cost of connecting flights is included in the calculation; on international flights, the cutoff is four hours rather than two. By the way, if, as a result of being bumped, you no longer want to go where you were going, you can get back twice the value of your ticket (or your money back plus $200, whichever is less).

Now about those delays. We're not talking about bumping

here, just the ordinary delays that crop up due to weather, equipment failure, and so on. If you're delayed for four hours or more, ask to see the airline's tariff book. (By law, they must show it to you.) Look under "delayed flights." You may well find that the airline is obliged to pay for your meals while you're waiting. If the delay occurs at night, they may also be obliged to pay for your overnight lodgings. Sometimes airline personnel will volunteer these amenities. Sometimes they won't, but they'll still provide them if you ask. If you think you're entitled to meals or lodging but the people you deal with at the airport refuse, you may be able to gain reimbursement later by writing the airline.

If your baggage is bruised, banged, broken, or lost, you again have rights. But the airline's liability is limited to $750 per passenger (not per bag). If you carry valuables in your luggage, you can purchase additional insurance from the airline. If you haven't purchased it, $750 is the most you can get. Naturally, if the airline thinks the damage was less, they'll offer you less.

If you have a problem in any of these areas, or any other problem with an airline, what you do depends on where you are. If the problem develops while you're at the airport, you'll be trying to get a quick solution. One of your major goals will be to speak with someone in authority. In the rushed atmosphere of a terminal, that can be difficult. Press underlings to let you talk to their superiors. Use the courtesy phones provided by some lines. Or resort to a pay phone, if necessary, to contact a person who can help you.

If you're no longer at the scene of the crime, and the damage has already been done, you have two principal lines of recourse. You can write to the airline's headquarters, or you can write to the Civil Aeronautics Board (see II-M).

Here are some addresses of major airline headquarters:

- American Airlines, PO Box 61616, Dallas/Fort Worth Airport, TX 75261
- Braniff International, Exchange Park, PO Box 35001, Dallas, TX 75235
- Continental Air Lines, Los Angeles International Airport, Los Angeles, CA 90009
- Delta Air Lines, Hartsfield Atlanta International Airport, Atlanta, GA 30320
- Eastern Air Lines, Miami International Airport, Miami, FL 33148
- National Airlines, Miami International Airport, Miami, FL 33159 (subsidiary of Pan American)
- Pan American World Airways, Pan American Building, 200 Park Ave., New York, NY 10017
- Republic Airlines, 7500 Airline Drive, Minneapolis, MN 55450
- Trans World Airlines, 605 Third Ave., New York, NY 10016
- United Air Lines, PO Box 66100, Chicago, IL 60666

If your letter to an airline fails to bring you fair treatment, complain to the Office of Consumer Affairs, Civil Aeronautics Board, 1825 Connecticut Ave. NW, Washington, DC 20428. The CAB has the final say on all complaints regarding the airlines. If it can't help you, your only further recourses are lawsuits and publicity.

Annuities. See Insurance.

Apartment-Location Services. Whenever housing is scarce in large cities, apartment-locating services spring up. They don't rent to anyone themselves. Rather, they match up prospective tenants with prospective landlords—for a fee. When apartments were plentiful, the fee was usually paid by the landlords. Now it's usually paid by the tenant. It may be a flat dollar sum, or (more often) be scaled to the rental of the apartment found. (The charge often runs from half a month's rent up to two months' rent.)

You might well grumble at having to pay the charge. But you wouldn't have grounds for complaint so long as the fees were openly stated, and so long as the agency really was instrumental in your finding the apartment in question. Unfortunately, some apartment-locating services have been downright underhanded. In New York and Chicago, for example, authorities cracked down on firms that were charging a fee in advance, and then referring prospective renters to apartments already occupied—or, in a couple of cases, torn down!

If an agency charges you for services it hasn't furnished or otherwise treats you unfairly, your best recourses are usually a city or county consumer protection agency if there is one in your area (see II-E); a Better Business Bureau (II-D); a state consumer protection agency (II-F); or a small claims court (II-N).

Apartments. See Landlord-Tenant Problems.

Appliances and Appliance Repairs. You say that your refrigerator's insides feel like a Florida beach? That your dishwasher or clothes washer is reluctant to trouble the dirt? That your dryer looks as if it's trying to do the latest dance step? Or maybe the trouble is with a trash compactor, humidifier, dehumidifier, freezer, oven, hot water heater, waste disposer, air conditioner, or range. All of these qualify as major appliances. Complaints about any of them may be sent to MACAP, the Major Appliance Consumer Action Panel, 20 N. Wacker Drive, Chicago, IL 60606.

MACAP was set up in 1970 by the major appliance manufacturers as a self-policing (and public relations) measure. It handles about twelve hundred complaints a year, and claims about 85 percent of them are resolved to the satisfaction of the consumer.

Don't bother to write MACAP unless you've already written to the retailer and the manufacturer, and haven't gotten satisfaction. That's the common sense way to handle it; it's also what MACAP insists on. If you write to MACAP first, the panel will simply refer your complaint back to the manufacturer.

Complaints to MACAP should include the appliance's brand name, model, and serial number; your name, address, and phone number; the date and place you bought the appliance; the name and address of the repair service involved (if it's different from the retailer's); and a description of what's wrong and the unsuccessful attempts to fix it. On receiving a complaint, MACAP asks the retailer and manufacturer to tell their side of the story within two weeks. Then it makes a "strong recommendation" for a solution.

Bess Myerson, former head of the New York City Department of Consumer Affairs, has said that the two-week deadline is sometimes breached and that some consumers find MACAP to be too lenient toward the manufacturer and retailer. Even so, she judged MACAP to be a remedy worth using and said the panel "has expedited an impressive number of consumer complaints."

What if MACAP fails to come up with a solution you consider fair? You still have other recourses, notably state consumer protection agencies (II-F) and small claims courts (II-N).

Here are the addresses of some major appliance manufacturers:

- Admiral Group (division of Rockwell International) 1701 E. Woodfield Road, Schaumburg, IL 60172
- Amana Refrigeration, Inc. (subsidiary of Raytheon Co.), Amana, IA 52204
- Frigidaire Division, General Motors Corp., 300 Taylor, Dayton, OH 45401
- General Electric Co., 3135 Easton Turnpike, Fairfield, CN 06431
- Kelvinator, Inc. (division of White Consolidated Industries), 4248 Kalamazoo St. SE, Grand Rapids, MI 49508
- Kenmore; house brand of Sears, Roebuck & Co., Sears Tower, Chicago, IL 60684
- KitchenAid Dishwasher Division, Hobart Manufacturing Co., World Headquarters Ave., Troy, OH 45374
- The Maytag Co., 403 W. 4th St., Newton, IA 50208
- Norge Division, Fedders Corp., Edison, NJ 08817
- Westinghouse Electric Corp., Westinghouse Building, Gateway Center—Box 2278, Pittsburgh, PA 15222
- Whirlpool Corp., Benton Harbor, MI 49022

Let's say your problem is not a major appliance but a small appliance. Then MACAP isn't a factor. You still start with the retailer and manufacturer, then proceed to a Better Business Bureau (II-D), and a state consumer protection agency (II-F).

If your beef is not with the appliance, but with the repair outfit sent to fix it, the dispute has a more local character. If complaining to the repair firm gets you nowhere, try a city or county agency (II-E), a Better Business Bureau (II-D), a state consumer agency (II-F), or a small claims court (II-N). Complaints about repairmen are common enough that there's likely to be a specialist at many complaint-handling agencies.

Audio and Audiovisual Equipment. See Televisions, Stereos, Radios, and Audiovisual Equipment and Repairs.

Automobile Repairs. (See also Automobile Sales.) Car repairs are without a doubt the nation's number-one consumer complaint. On my own Gripe Index, based on my 1975 survey of state consumer protection agencies, car repairs scored 97 out of a possible 100. (Car sales were second with 83, and home improvements and repairs third with 65. For a complete rundown on the Gripe Index, see Appendix I.) In short, if you've got auto headaches, you're not alone.

In 1979, the U.S. Department of Transportation sent teams of undercover investigators to sixty-two randomly picked repair shops in seven areas (Atlanta, Brooklyn, Houston, Miami, Nashville, Philadelphia, and White Plains). The teams drove their cars into the repair shops and asked to have them fixed. Result: About 53 percent of the charges were for needless work. Also, between 11 percent of the time (in the case of brakes) and 31 percent of the time (suspensions) the defect didn't get fixed.

Similar results have been reported by many investigative teams. When *The New York Times* tried it in 1975 (in conjunction with the Suffolk County Dept. of Consumer Affairs), thirteen of twenty-four repair shops either misdiagnosed the problem, or performed or recommended expensive and unnecessary repairs. Surveys in Michigan, California, and elsewhere have come up with similar findings.

Before we talk about what to do about your auto-repair problem, let's say a word about two measures that *might* help keep it from happening again. First, try to find a NIASE-certified mechanic in your area, NIASE being the National Institute for Automotive Service Excellence. Mechanics who have this distinction are allowed to advertise it; watch for such ads when you pass gas stations or repair shops. Otherwise, you can do a phone survey of repair shops in your area to see which ones, if any, have NIASE-certified mechanics. As of early 1980, about 29 percent of full-time mechanics had NIASE certification in one or more repair specialties. About 6 percent of full-time mechanics were certified by NIASE as "general automobile mechanics," having passed tests in all eight auto-repair specialties in the NIASE program.

Second, you might want to check with the American Automobile Association (AAA) affiliate in your area to see if they have an "approved auto repair" program in your area. Under this program, the AAA selects certain auto repair shops, recommends them to its members, and requires that any disputes be given to AAA arbitrators for binding arbitration.

In any case, let's say that you're stuck with an auto repair problem. What do you do now? Let's break the problem down into four areas: (1) a brand-new car; (2) problems with a car under warranty; (3) problems with a car no longer under warranty; and (4) body work.

If your problem is with a brand-new car, see the discussion of what to do with a lemon under Automobile sales.

If your problem is with a car under warranty, your basic trouble may be that you're getting the "sunshine treatment," also known as the sunbath or parking-lot treatment. By whatever name, it's the procedure whereby the dealer takes your car in, lets it sit in the lot all day, and proclaims it fixed. Dealers may be tempted to do this because of the economics of the warranty system. The dealer's reimbursement comes not from you but from the manufacturer. The dealer may perhaps consider this reimbursement inadequate, in which case warranty repairs become a stepchild at that dealership. In any case, the manufacturer's reimbursement is based on the dealer's report of the repair. Unless you complain, there's no way the manufacturer can learn that the work was not done. It's only going to see an invoice from the dealer claiming that things were fixed. (There have even been a few dealers who have set up rackets, bilking manufacturers by billing them for thousands of dollars in phony repairs. These, of course, represent an extreme.) Of course, there are dealers whose pride and desire for repeat business encourage them to run high-quality repair operations, even if many warranty repairs are done at a loss. But if you have found one of these upstanding dealers, you are probably not reading this passage.

Your basic weapons against sunshine treatment are good records, persistence, and assertiveness. Keep meticulous records, especially during the warranty period, of anything that goes wrong with your car and of every effort to fix it. Thus armed, you can take several steps. *Step one* is to try to deal with the top person at the dealership, if you feel you're getting a runaround from subordinates.

If you don't get satisfaction at the dealer's, *step two* is to write to the manufacturer. I suggest writing the president of the manufacturer, with a copy to the zone office. (The address of the zone office is usually in the owner's manual, or can be obtained from the dealer.) You'll usually end up dealing with zone office personnel, but writing to headquarters may give you better leverage.

The headquarters of the four major American automobile manufacturers are:

- American Motors Corp., 27777 Franklin Road, Southfield, MI 48634
- Chrysler Corp., 1200 Lynn Townsend Dr., Detroit, MI 48231
- Ford Motor Co., The American Road, Dearborn, MI 48121
- General Motors Corp., 3044 W. Grand Blvd., Detroit, MI 48202

U.S. headquarters addresses for some major foreign car manufacturers are:

- American Honda Motor Co., 100 W. Alondra, Gardena, CA 90247
- Nissan Motor Corp., USA (Datsun), 18501 S. Figueroa St., Carson, CA 90744
- Toyota Motor Sales, USA, Inc., 2055 W. 190th St., Torrance, CA 90509
- Subaru of America, Inc., 7040 Central Highway, Pennsauken, NJ 08109
- Volkswagen of America, 818 Sylvan Ave., Englewood Cliffs, NJ 07632

The two largest U.S. manufacturers, GM and Ford, have been experimenting recently with new methods for resolving consumer disputes. In 1978, General Motors started a pilot program in the Minneapolis area, featuring binding arbitration under the auspices of the Better Business Bureau. The program went statewide in 1979, and further expansion was planned. Ford instituted what it called the Ford Consumer Appeals Board in 1977 in North Carolina. The board is a five-person panel, with two industry representatives and three consumer representatives. In less than a year, the Ford panel received some 1,600 calls, resulting in 171 formal cases. The first 110 cases reviewed resulted in decisions favoring the dealer in 68 cases, and in decisions favoring the consumer in 30 cases, according to *The New York Times*. The panel's decisions are binding on the dealer but not on the consumer. (By contrast, the GM plan in Minnesota is binding on both sides.)

Between 1977 and early 1980, Ford set up six more consumer appeals boards, for New Jersey; Washington and Oregon; Maryland and the District of Columbia; Virginia; and California. (There are two boards in California, one in Los Angeles and one in San Francisco.) All of the boards follow the original pattern, with three consumer representatives and two business representatives. The consumer representation is genuine: For example, the Southern California board includes the president of the Consumer Federation of California and the director of the Office of Consumer Affairs in Santa Ana. A Ford spokesperson said that more than 23 percent of Ford, Lincoln, and Mercury owners now live in an area served by one of the boards.

If your negotiations with the dealer hit a dead end, *step three* is to try an AUTOCAP, if there's one in your area. AUTOCAPs are organizations set up specifically to deal with consumer complaints about cars and car dealers. They were cofounded by the federal Office of Consumer Affairs, the National Automobile Dealers Association, and other trade groups. An AUTOCAP first tries mediation. If that fails, it assembles a panel, consisting of both dealers and consumer group representatives, to hear your case and render a judgment. The opinion carries considerable weight, but isn't legally binding.

A recent tally showed twenty-one AUTOCAPS operating in eighteen states, usually under the auspices of a dealers' association.

- In Connecticut: Connecticut Automotive Trades Association, 18 N. Main Street, West Hartford, CT 06107
- In Delaware: Delaware Automobile Dealers Association, 8 Hillvale Circle, Wilmington, DE 19808
- In Georgia: Georgia Automobile Dealers Association, 1380 W. Paces Ferry Road, Suite 230, Atlanta, GA 30327
- In Idaho: Idaho Automobile Dealers Association, 2230 Main St., Boise, ID 83706
- In Indiana: Indianapolis Automobile Trade Association, 7100 Lakewood Building, Suite 210 E, 5987 E. 71st, Indianapolis, IN 46220
- In Kentucky: Kentucky Automobile Dealers Association,

PO Box 498, Frankfort, KY 40601; and Greater Louisville Auto Dealers Association, 1103 Heyburn Building, 332 W. Broadway, Louisville, KY 40202

- In Louisiana: Louisiana Automobile Dealers Association, PO Box 2863, Baton Rouge, LA 70821; and Greater New Orleans New Car Dealers Association, 811 International Building, New Orleans, LA 70130
- In Maryland: Automotive Trade Association, National Capital Area, 8401 Connecticut Ave., Suite 505, Chevy Chase, MD 20015
- In Massachusetts: Massachusetts State Auto Dealers Association, 437 Boylston St., Boston, MA 02116
- In Michigan: Michigan Automobile Dealers Association, 1500 Kendale Blvd., PO Box 860, East Lansing, MI 48823
- In New York: Niagara Frontier Automobile Dealers Association, 25 California Drive, Williamsville, NY 14221
- In Ohio: Cleveland Automobile Dealers Association, 310 Lakeside Ave., West Cleveland, OH 44113; and Toledo Automobile Dealers Association, 1811 North Reynolds, Toledo, OH 43615
- In Oklahoma: Oklahoma Automobile Dealers Association, 1601 City National Bank Tower, Oklahoma City, OK 73102
- In Oregon: Oregon Automobile Dealers Association, PO Box 14460, Portland, OR 97214
- In Pennsylvania: AutoCAP, York County Consumer Protection Office, Courthouse, 28 Market St., York, PA 17401
- In Texas: Texas Automobile Dealers Association, PO Drawer 1028, 1108 Lavaca, Austin, TX 78767
- In Utah: Utah Automobile Dealers Association, Newhouse Hotel, Box 1019, Salt Lake City, UT 84101
- In Virginia: Virginia Automobile Dealers Association, 1800 W. Grace St., Box 5407, Richmond, VA 23220

If there's no AUTOCAP near you in the above list, check with the National Automobile Dealers Association, 8400 West Park Drive, McLean, VA 22101, to see if one's been recently established in your area. If there's no AUTOCAP where you live, NADA can tell you whether the local dealers' association has another sort of program to handle consumer complaints.

If you can't gain satisfaction through an AUTOCAP or dealers' group, your logical *step four* is probably a complaint to your state consumer protection agency (see II-F), city or county consumer protection agency (II-E), or Better Business Bureau (II-D). If none of those avenues works, you have to turn to *step five,* legal action (see II-N, O and P). You may need to move from one corrective measure to the next faster than you normally would, if one of your goals is to get needed repairs done while the warranty's still in force.

One drastic form of legal action, which you should keep in mind as a last resort, is revoking acceptance of your car. The procedure for doing this is described in the discussion of automobile sales, because you'd be most likely to try it with a brand-new car that turned out to be a lemon. However, revoking acceptance can also be done with a car that's seen some use. An Alabama man once revoked acceptance on a car he'd had for nearly a year, after driving it some twenty thousand miles. A court upheld his action, saying that it was only the constant promises from the dealer that everything would be straightened out that caused the man to keep the car so long.

So much for repairs under warranty. Now let's take the situation where the warranty's expired. It's a different ball game now, because *you're* paying for the repairs. Your most likely concern now is not that the repair shop is doing too little, but that it's doing too much—or at least charging you for too much.

You'll notice we switched to saying "repair shop" instead of "dealer." Once the warranty expires, you're free to get your repairs wherever you choose. We've already mentioned that it might pay you to choose a place with a NIASE-certified mechanic, or one approved by the local AAA. A check with the local Better Business Bureau, or even with your friends and neighbors, might also keep you from driving into the jaws of financial disaster. As a rule, repair shops on local streets are to be preferred to those next to major highways: The local places depend more on repeat business, and have greater incentive to do a workmanlike job. If you find a mechanic you like, patronize the place regularly, for gas as well as for repairs. The better you know people at a gas station or repair shop, the more likely they are to take that special measure of care reserved for a friend or steady customer.

Generally, you should prefer shops that provide a written estimate of repair charges in advance. And you should always ask for an estimate, unless you've worked with a particular repair shop many times, and trust its people completely.

In some states (including California, Connecticut, Maryland, New York, and Rhode Island) and cities (including New York, Dallas, and Washington DC) auto repair shops are licensed. If you have a problem, you can complain to the city or state agency in charge of licensing.

If repair shops aren't licensed in your area, the logical places to complain are the Better Business Bureau (see II-D); city or county consumer protection agency, if any (II-E); and state consumer protection agency (II-F). An action line (II-T) may be able to help. A last resort might be picketing, or other unconventional tactics (II-Z).

Now about body work. Sigh. There are few things more disheartening than the sight of crumpled steel when your car's been hit. But pull yourself together, because you confront a triangle—you, the repair shop, and your insurance company. Your interests are not quite the same as the insurance company's. The insurer's interest is primarily in seeing that the car gets fixed as cheaply as possible. Your interest is primarily in seeing that it gets fixed right. If both parties are responsible, you'll see the other's point of view, but there's still some potential conflict there.

The insurance company may well suggest a place you can go to get the work done. (This is legal in almost all states.) The adjuster will tell you that Joe's Wham-Bam Auto Body Shop does good work, and does it fast. He may add that Joe has agreed to do the work based on a predetermined pay scale set by the insurance company. (Even if he doesn't add that, it may be true.) You've never heard of Joe's Wham-Bam Auto Body Shop before, so what should you do?

Pick your own body shop. Joe's might do fine work. But then again it might be tempted to do high-volume, low-quality work. In exchange for a steady stream of clients fed to it by the insurance company, Joe's may keep prices at bargain-basement levels—but then your car may look as though it's been fixed in a bargain basement.

You make the decision as to what body shop to use. As with repair shops, take recommendations from friends and check with the local Better Business Bureau. Get an estimate from the shop of your choice. "It's too high," the insurance adjuster may say. Let the adjuster bargain with the shop. The shop is not about to take a loss, so any figure it agrees to is probably fair. If the insurer and the shop can't agree on a figure, you should offer to get other estimates—again, from body shops you choose. If the insurance company reaches an impasse with two or three shops, it's time to start writing letters. Send one to your state insurance department (see addresses under Insurance), and one to your consumer protection agency (II-F).

The insurance company may give you a check early in the game in the amount it thinks is fair. That's all right—but don't cash the check yet. Cashing it often constitutes your agreement to the amount of the settlement. Instead, hold on to the check until all the repair work is done to your satisfaction and the final bill is submitted. Then, if the check still seems like a fair settlement, go ahead and cash it.

What if the quality of the body work isn't up to snuff? Assuming you chose the shop, you can't expect the insurance company to ante up extra money for more repairs. Rather, you should insist that the shop do the work right at the price you originally agreed upon. In this kind of dispute with a body shop, your recourses are the typical ones for local complaints: city or county agencies (II-E), state agencies (II-F), Better Business Bureaus, including their arbitration services (II-D), small claims courts (II-N), and voluntary consumer groups (II-Q).

Automobile Sales. "If you have a lemon," the saying goes, "make lemonade." Easier said than done. But we'll try.

The best way to make sure a car is delivered to you in the condition you want is to refuse to accept it—or pay for it—until everything is just right. This, however, requires steely self-control and an alternate mode of transportation. If you take the car with some defects remaining to be corrected, sit down right away and send a letter to the dealer, keeping at least one photocopy (not just a carbon copy; this letter may have to be reproduced later). The letter should say something to this effect:

> I today purchased from you, at a cost of [amount], a [year, make, and model] with the serial number [whatever]. On delivery, it had three defects of which I was immediately aware. Paint on the right front door is chipped. The glove compartment is difficult to open.

> And an AM radio was installed instead of the AM-FM unit I had ordered and paid for. You will recall our discussion of this morning, in which you said these defects will be remedied as soon as possible. Please advise me when I can bring the car in for the necessary adjustments. I would appreciate your selecting a time before [a specified time]. I appreciate your prompt attention to these matters, and will let you know if any other defects manifest themselves.

Any time another defect does show up, write the dealer again, taking the opportunity to remind him of any previous defects that haven't been corrected yet. Your letters won't necessarily bring you any faster service than phone calls would. Indeed, you may want to supplement them with phone calls. But your letters will create a written record, which could be invaluable in any subsequent disputes.

If the dealer is excessively tardy in setting your car to rights, your potential recourses include an AUTOCAP (see Automobile Repairs), a dealers' association (see name entry), a Better Business Bureau (see II-D), a city or county consumer agency (II-E), or a state cosumer agency (II-F).

If the car is a complete and utter lemon, to the point where you can see that living with it would be pure torture, you can use the most extreme weapon available to you—revoking your acceptance of the car. This step will normally land you in court, and should be done only in consultation with a lawyer. For a detailed discussion of how to do it, see the book *What to Do with Your Bad Car: An Action Manual for Lemon Owners,* by Ralph Nader, Lowell Dodge, and Ralf Hotchkiss. In essence, the procedure works like this. You write a letter saying, "In accordance with Section 2-608 of the Uniform Commercial Code, I am hereby revoking my acceptance of [the car, whose model and serial number you give], purchased from you on [date] for the sum of [amount]."

You should go on to describe the defects you can't live with and that the dealer and manufacturer have been unable to rectify. Also note the car's current mileage. Then you should demand return of the purchase price of the car.

The letter should be sent by certified mail, return receipt requested. You should keep a photocopy (again, not a carbon copy).

Almost certainly, the dealer will refuse to take the car back. In preparation for legal action, you should take a number of steps. By noting the mileage at the time the car is returned to the dealer, you lay the groundwork for a future contention that the dealer has "exercised dominion" over the vehicle (if the mileage later is significantly higher). To show that you mean business, you should cancel your insurance on the car and your registration. Notify the dealer in writing that you've done these things.

If you're making payments on the car, the procedure becomes more complex. Get detailed advice from your lawyer and be sure that any finance company or bank involved gets a copy of all communications you send the dealer.

Revoking acceptance is, to repeat, an extreme measure. You'll want to use it only as a last resort, since it can involve you in tremendous red tape, and possible financial loss. So, exhaust your more conventional remedies first. If it looks like you may have to revoke acceptance, have your lawyer send the dealer a note (on the lawyer's stationery) saying that you are preparing to revoke acceptance. If you're fortunate, this in itself may precipitate some last-minute action that results in a satisfactory solution.

Of course, being stuck with a lemon isn't the only problem that can crop up with a car dealer. Another problem that occurs fairly often is a hassle in which you believe the dealer isn't living up to his promises. The best way to avoid these "misunderstandings" is to get everything in writing before you buy, including (1) the delivery date; (2) the exact list of options you're buying; (3) the list of things the dealer will do to make the car ready, often known as "dealer prep"; (4) the terms of the financing, if you're doing it through the dealer; and (5) the exact cost, including options, dealer preparation, shipping, taxes, and financing. The dealer should sign a statement that there will be no other charges.

Nailing things down that way will help keep last-minute charges from cropping up. Protective undercoating, for example, is a favorite way for some dealers to tack on a few more dollars. But it's often included on the dealer preparation checklist, which means you supposedly have already paid for it. Anyway, undercoating—other than what's done at the factory—is usually unnecessary, according to Consumers Union, the prestigious nonprofit testing organization. If a dispute comes up, it's still not too late to ask to see a copy of the dealer preparation checklist. There's certainly no reason you should pay twice for the same item.

Financing is another area in which consumers often have gripes against car dealers. But the complaints typically concern oral misrepresentation, which is the dickens to prove. For example, dealers sometimes quote seemingly low interest rates, when the actual annual percentage rate is much higher. (This practice is much less common than it used to be, but it still happens occasionally.) If you have a complaint of this type, send it to your state consumer protection agency (see II-F), the Better Business Bureau (II-D), and the Federal Trade Commission (II-H), which administers the Truth in Lending Act. All of this probably won't do you any good, if you've signed a contract. But the BBB can warn other potential victims, and the other two agencies might launch an investigation if they get a number of complaints against a dealership. You'll probably be stuck making the payments you've agreed, in writing, to make. If you can't make them, see the entry on Debt Collection for a description of your rights.

Used cars pose a tougher situation, since you normally get no guarantee of a used car's mechanical condition. (The Federal Trade Commission has proposed changes in this situation, but I doubt the FTC's proposals will become reality, at least for some years.) Your rights when you buy a used car are pretty well limited to whatever is spelled out in any warranty or written agreement you've gotten from the seller. (The warranties are usually token items, except when you pay an additional fee for more extended warranty coverage.)

When buying a used car, you can do a few things that may help prevent trouble. Test drive the car. Have it inspected by an impartial mechanic (yours). If your state has an inspection system, take the car through the state inspection line. Also, ask the dealer for the name of the previous owner (the dealer always has a record of this, whether he'll admit it or not), and talk with that person. Taking any or all of these precautions may help keep you from getting stung.

If you are stung nevertheless, your recourses include AUTOCAPs, dealers' associations, the Better Business Bureau (see II-D), city or county agencies (II-E), state consumer agencies (II-F), and small claims court (II-N).

Bait and Switch. This form of unfair business practice probably predates written history, but it's still going strong. The seller offers what looks like a bargain. When you go to buy it, he or she substitutes a higher-priced item.

Example: A department store had a sale on "personal size" nine-inch black-and-white television sets. Only $68, according to the ad in the paper. A young man we'll call Phil walked in to buy one. "Those TVs," said the salesman, "have to be specially ordered. We can get you one, but you'll have to wait a few weeks."

"A few weeks!" exclaimed Phil. "But they're on sale. The ad's in the paper today!"

Sorry, said the salesman, but each store only had one of those sets on hand, for demonstration. If Phil wanted a set right now, he could select a twelve-inch model that also happened to be on sale. Only $80.

That's bait and switch. The bait is the low-priced offer. When you go for the bait, the salesperson either starts to disparage the advertised item ("Oh, that one's not really too good, but *this* one over *here* . . .") or tells you it's not available right now. He tries to "trade you up" to a more expensive item, whose good qualities and immediate availability know no bounds.

Bait-and-switch tactics are illegal in virtually every state, either by explicit statute or under the state's unfair and deceptive trade practices act. Some cities also have ordinances banning bait-and-switch tactics. Furthermore, the Federal Trade Commission has had guidelines against what it calls "bait advertising" since 1959. (The FTC rules can be used against any merchant big enough to "affect" interstate commerce.) So, if you encounter bait-and-switch tactics, complain to your local consumer protection agency (see II-E), state consumer agency (II-F), and the nearest office of the FTC (II-H). Also register your gripe with the newspaper, radio station, or TV station that carried the ad. It may think twice about taking ads from the offending business in the future.

Postscript—about Phil. He was not your average, doormat-variety consumer. He didn't know exactly where to complain, but he knew bait-and-switch tactics were illegal. So he called the police. Much commotion followed. When the dust had settled, Phil left the store with a television that normally cost $89.99, having paid for it the sum of $68. "The television works beautifully," he reported. "I just love it."

Banks. You're turned down for a loan, and you don't think the decision was fair. Or there's a mistake in your balance, and despite your three phone calls, the same mistake has now appeared on your monthly statement two months in a row. Or you believe a local bank is engaging in redlining, refusing to grant mortgage loans in a particular neighborhood.

These are some of the complaints you might have about a bank. Contrary to folklore, bankers don't all have hearts of granite. Don't overlook the obvious—talking the problem over with a top-level official of the bank.

If that doesn't work, there are a number of specialized regulatory agencies you can turn to. But you can hardly tell the agencies without a scorecard. In many cases, the simplest approach is to ask officials of the bank what regulatory agency they report to. That question may have the side benefit of getting bank officials to take your complaint a bit more seriously.

Which agency regulates your bank depends on a few variables. First, you have to know what type of banking institution you're dealing with. There are (1) commercial banks, (2) savings and loan associations, (3) mutual savings banks, and (4) credit unions. Second, you have to know whether the institution you're complaining about is state chartered or federally chartered.

Let's say your problem is with a commercial bank. Then your complaint should normally go to one of three federal agencies—the Comptroller of the Currency, the Federal Reserve System, or the Federal Deposit Insurance Corporation (FDIC). Which one? Well, that's what you need the scorecard for. Here it is.

The Comptroller of the Currency regulates national banks. Of the 14,600 commercial banks in the United States (as of early 1980), about 4,600 are national banks. Usually, a national bank will have the word "national" somewhere in its name; sometimes the initials N. A. Address your complaint about a national bank to the Consumer Affairs Section, Comptroller of the Currency, U.S. Department of the Treasury, Washington DC 20220.

The Federal Reserve System regulates about 1,000 commercial banks. These are commercial banks that are state chartered but are nevertheless members of the Federal Reserve System. (All national banks are members automatically.) Again, the best way to tell if your bank is one of these is to ask. Send complaints to the Director, Division of Consumer Affairs, Board of Governors of the Federal Reserve System, Washington DC 20551.

The Federal Deposit Insurance Corporation (FDIC) regulates some 8,800 commercial banks that are state chartered, are not members of the Federal Reserve System, and carry federal deposit insurance. (About 60 percent of commercial banks meet this description.) Send complaints about these banks to the Office of Consumer Affairs and Civil Rights, Federal Deposit Insurance Corp., 550 Seventeenth St. NW, Washington DC 20429.

If you've been doing the arithmetic as you went along, you've noticed that there are still a couple of hundred banks that aren't answerable to any of these three federal agencies. These are state-chartered banks that do not carry federal deposit insurance. With these banks, your only recourse is to the state banking department.

You can also complain to the state banking department about any problem you have with a state-chartered bank— even if it's also subject to one of the federal agencies discussed above. All fifty states have agencies that regulate state-chartered banking institutions. You can find their names and addresses in the phone book, or by checking at your public library, or by calling a general information number for state government offices. Usually the agency is called the Department of Banking, Division of Banking, Commissioner of Banking, Banking Department, or Superintendent of Banking.

In Indiana and Utah, it's the Department of Financial Institutions; in Louisiana, the Office of Financial Institutions. In Missouri, it's the Division of Finance in the Department of Consumer Affairs, Regulation and Licensing. In Hawaii, it's the Bank Examination Division, Department of Regulatory Agencies. In Idaho, it's the Department of Finance. In Maine, it's the Bureau of Banking within the Department of Business Regulation; in Montana, it's the Financial Division within the same department. In Michigan, it's the Financial Institutions Bureau. In South Carolina, it's the Consumer Finance Division in the Board of Financial Institutions. In Virginia, it's the Bureau of Banking within the Corporation Commission. In Wyoming, it's the Office of State Examiner.

What if your problem isn't with a commercial bank? If the institution is state chartered, the same state agencies still apply. In addition, you may be able to call upon a federal agency for help. For that, you need a new scorecard.

Savings and loan associations and mutual savings banks both fall under the heading of savings institutions. If they're federally chartered, the word "federal" will appear somewhere in their name. Complaints against these institutions go to the Consumer Division, Office of Community Investment, Federal Home Loan Bank Board, Washington, DC 20552.

If a savings institution is state chartered but carries federal insurance, you can write to the Federal Savings and Loan Insurance Corp. (FSLIC) at the same address.

If a savings institution is state chartered and doesn't carry federal deposit insurance, then your only recourse is to state banking authorities.

With credit unions, it's pretty straightforward. Those that are federally chartered will have the word "federal" in their name. To complain about any federally chartered credit union, write the National Credit Union Administration, Washington, DC 20456. For state-chartered credit unions, your state banking department is the place to go.

Basement Waterproofing. See Home Improvements and Repairs.

Billing. (See also Credit Problems; Debt Collection.) Basically, there are three irksome things people can do to you when they're billing you for a product or service. They can bill you for the wrong amount. They can give you insufficient time to pay. Or they can calculate your bill in a way that's unfavorable to you. You have some remedies for each of these problems.

Let's say you get billed for the wrong amount. Obviously, the first thing you do is write back and state that the bill's in error, according to your records. (Ordinarily, you should also pay the portion that's not in dispute.) Unfortunately, it's not unusual for a company to ignore (or take forever to process) your letter, so that you continue to get dunning letters. The dunning notes may get increasingly insistent.

Part of your frustration in these situations may stem from your feeling that you're dealing with a computer, not with another human being. Companies sometimes encourage you to feel this way: When they make a goof, they blame it on "computer problems," or say "our computer entered the wrong figure in your account." This is baloney. Computers are simply tools. Before computers were widely used, would you have been soothed with the assurance that "our adding machine made a mistake"? Of course not. And the statement that a computer erred is the same sort of silly statement. Computers aren't responsible for their actions. The people who run them are. What you want to do is communicate with the people who are hiding behind the machine. If you know the name of a company official, use it. If you can find out the name (at the library, for example), do so. If you don't know anyone's name, write to the director of the billing department.

I know how frustrating all this can be. The ritual of aggravation so irked one fellow I know (a New York editor, normally urbane and calm) that he started sending the dunning notes back with obscene messages scrawled on them in red ink. Their gist was that the company should take its bill and store it in an interior portion of its anatomy.

You may not be driven so far. If the bill is from a credit card issuer, the Fair Credit Billing Act requires the creditor to respond to billing inquiries within thirty days, and to straighten them out within ninety days. If you need help enforcing the law, start with the regional office of the Federal Trade Commission (see II-H).

Under the Fair Credit Billing Act, if the creditor doesn't resolve the dispute within ninety days (either by correcting its bill or explaining why it's right and you're wrong), the creditor forfeits any right to the disputed amount, up to $50.

Some states have laws that go farther than that, in that they apply to most creditors (not just credit card issuers), or in that they have limits higher than $50. For information on state laws in this regard, contact your state consumer protection agency (see II-F).

Now for the second problem—a bill that arrives Tuesday and demands payment by Wednesday (or, worse, Monday). The Fair Credit Billing Act also has some standards that apply here. It says a bill must be postmarked at least fourteen days before finance charges become due. Make sure you keep the envelope with the postmark. Again, there may be additional protection for you under state law.

The third problem—unfavorable billing methods—is tricky. You may have it without knowing you have it. That's because most consumers are in the dark concerning how their charge account bills are calculated. They know they're billed 18 percent a year, or 1.5 percent a month. But 1.5 percent of *what?* Most consumers don't really know. "My balance," they'd say. But there are several ways of calculating the balance.

The best method, from the consumer's point of view, is the "unpaid balance" method, also known as the "previous balance less payments" method. If you had a $200 balance at the start of a billing period but have since paid in $100, you would be charged interest only on the remaining $100 under this method. That means your finance charge for the month would probably be $1.50. The finance charge would be the same even if you've meanwhile charged the purchase of a $50 table.

The worst method, from the consumer's viewpoint, is the "previous balance" method. With it, you'd be charged interest on the whole $200, so your finance charge would probably be $3.00. The previous balance method is now outlawed in a number of states, but there are still plenty of places where it's used. Once you get in the habit of checking to see what kind of computation methods are used on your bills, you can outlaw previous balance creditors from your personal financial domain.

Two in-between methods, in terms of their favorability to you, are the "adjusted balance" method and the "average daily balance" method. With the adjusted balance method, your finance charge takes account of both payments and purchases you've made since the last statement. So, in the situation described above, your balance would be $150. (That's $200 to start with, minus the $100 payment, plus the $50 for purchase of the table.) Your finance charge would probably be $2.25.

With the average daily balance method, the balance on which you pay your interest is, as the name implies, the average of the balances you maintained on each day of the billing cycle. How favorable this method is to you depends on whether you are charged interest on a purchase starting the moment you buy it, or whether you get a "free ride" until after you've been billed for the purchase. This free ride period has been one of the main features making the use of credit cards worthwhile. But some card issuers have started doing away with it.

How important to you is all this? Well, if you carry a credit card balance of $2,000, the way your finance charge is calculated can easily make a difference to you of $30 a month.

What, then, should you do about it? Start by learning what method is being used on any and all credit cards you have. Many stores and other card issuers have been quietly changing their balance methods in recent years, to help *their* balance sheets and hurt yours. Once you know what method is being used, you can complain to the card issuer if you think it's unfair. If enough people do that, the issuer might change its method. In the meantime, you can safeguard your own checkbook by switching to a competing card, or simply by dropping that particular credit card. If a store or card issuer uses a method that you believe is unfair, you may also want to write to the Federal Trade Commission (II-H) or to your elected representatives (II-V) to work toward the outlawing of that method.

One more billing problem should be mentioned here. If you have a bank card or a general-purpose charge card, you may use it sometime to buy merchandise that proves defective. When your bill comes, you may be in a quandary as to whether or not to pay. Your quarrel is with the merchant, not the card issuer. But if you pay, you rightly fear you may never see your money again. The answer, since the passage of the Fair Credit Billing Act, is *don't pay* the disputed portion. See the entry on Credit Problems for further details.

Bonds. See Securities.

Book Clubs. See Buying Clubs.

Builders. See Home Improvements and Repairs; Houses.

Buses. If you have a problem with a bus line, your first recourse is whichever employee you can grab; your second is the manager of the terminal, if you can find him; your third is the bus company headquarters. Headquarters addresses for two of the biggest bus companies are:

- Greyhound Lines, Inc., Greyhound Tower, Phoenix, AZ 85077
- National Trailways Bus System, 1200 I Street NW, Washington DC 20005

If the company doesn't give you satisfaction, your principal recourse is the Interstate Commerce Commission (see II-L). The ICC's not known as a consumer's best friend, but I hope they'll surprise you.

One other agency you might try, if you can find it, is the state agency that regulates intrastate transportation. Your state public utilities commission (see Utilities and Utility Bills) may have this responsibility, or may be able to tell you who does.

Business Opportunities. (See also Distributorships; Franchises.) "Do you write songs? We'll market them for you. Pay us a modest fee of $50 and we'll arrange for your songs to be looked at by major musical and publishing houses." That (fictitious) ad capsulizes in brief form what's wrong with many business opportunities. The promises are vague; only the fee you pay is definite. In fact, if you get caught in a phony business opportunity, you'll be lucky if $50 is all you lose. Many of these situations are "opportunities" for the person who gets your money, but not necessarily for you. All too often you pay for help in getting started in some business, but receive only token or desultory help—or none at all.

In getting involved with any business venture, you should know exactly whom you're getting in with, what their past record is, and exactly what they're committed—on paper, in a signed contract—to do for you.

If you've leaped before you looked, one place from which you may be able to get help is the Inspection Service of the U.S. Postal Service—the outfit that investigates mail fraud. The real crooks in the business opportunity racket often use post office boxes and ask you to send money through the mail. (So, of course, do some legitimate operators.) That means that the postal inspectors have an entry to get involved on your behalf. They can often be aggressive and effective in gathering evidence for the prosecution of mail fraud, and in helping to get your money back.

You can contact the Inspection Service in any of three ways—through your local postmaster, through your local postal inspector, or by writing Chief Postal Inspector, U.S. Postal Service, Room 3517, Washington, DC 20260.

If mail fraud isn't involved, the agencies that are the best bets for getting some of your money back are usually the state consumer agency (see II-F) and/or the state attorney general's office (which may or may not be distinct from the consumer agency). Other recourses include city and county agencies (II-E), small claims court (II-N), threatening a lawsuit (II-O), and, if a large sum's at stake, actually instituting a lawsuit (II-P).

Buying Clubs. "I can get it for you wholesale." That time-honored claim is the whole basis of buying clubs. By being a member, it is claimed, you can get cars, books, records, coins, magazines, or general merchandise at prices well below what you'd normally expect to pay. By the time you add in the membership fees or shipping charges, this claim may turn out to be wishful thinking. But even if it is true, you may end up with merchandise you wouldn't normally have bought. In that case, the savings are real in a bookkeeping sense but all too illusory in the pocketbook.

Before joining a buying club, it's wise to inquire about (1) annual or one-time membership fees, (2) the number of items, or dollar volume, you're required to purchase, (3) mailing, shipping, or handling charges that may come up, (4) "negative option" plans, and (5) the sending of merchandise "on approval."

A negative option plan is an arrangement by which you'll be sent the club's selection of merchandise unless you specifically request not to be sent it. FTC regulations require that you be given at least ten days to decide whether you want a particular selection. Even so, over a period of time, the effect of a negative option plan is often to cause you to "order" merchandise you never would have gone out and bought.

Merchandise that is sent on approval theoretically can be accepted or rejected by you. But if you reject it, you sometimes have to ship it back at your own cost. Some buying clubs send items "on approval" without making it clear in advance exactly what you're going to receive or how you can return if it you don't want it. Sometimes the term "on approval" isn't explained, so that the consumer doesn't realize until too late that he's expected to pay for the merchandise, even though he may not specifically have ordered it.

If you've already joined a buying club, but one or more of these key conditions weren't made clear to you when you joined, you may be able to bow out and get some or all of your money back. Send a complaint letter to the president of the club, explaining your desire to withdraw from the club, to get a refund, or both. Send a copy of your letter to your state consumer protection agency or agencies (see II-F). Send another copy to your local Better Business Bureau (II-D), and to your city or county consumer protection agency, if you have one (II-E). If the club operates by mail, also send a copy to the Postal Inspector in Charge at the nearest regional office of the U.S. Postal Service.

Carpeting. There used to be a consumer action panel for carpeting (called CRICAP and run by the Carpet and Rug Institute) comparable to AUTOCAPs (see Automobile Repairs) and MACAP (see Appliances and Appliance Repairs). Unfortunately, it folded in 1975 for lack of financial support.

If your initial complaints to the retailer and manufacturer have proved fruitless, though, you can still write CRICAP's sponsor, the Carpet and Rug Institute, at PO Box 2048 (Holiday Drive), Dalton, GA 30720.

If the institute can't bring your problem to a satisfactory solution, you should decide who you think is really at fault, the retailer or the manufacturer. If it's the retailer, complaints to the Better Business Bureau (see II-D), your local consumer protection agency (II-E), and your state consumer protection agency (II-F) are in order. Perhaps you can press the retailer to have your dispute arbitrated by a Better Business Bureau panel. Or you can go to small claims court (II-N).

If you figure it's the manufacturer who's really to blame and the Carpet and Rug Institute hasn't been able to help, send a complaint letter to the consumer protection agency in the manufacturer's state, as well as to your own state agency.

Cars. See Automobile Repairs; Automobile Sales.

Clothing. Most garments now come with permanent care labels attached. If you don't follow the label's instructions and your garment rips, deteriorates, puckers, or otherwise self-destructs, you don't have much of a case. But if you have given it proper care and no more than reasonable wear, and if one of these things *still* happens, that's another story. Fixing the garment is probably impossible at this point, so what you're after is either a replacement or a refund. (Decide in advance which one you want, and then stick to your guns.)

If you've been washing the garment yourself and it falls apart prematurely, your first complaint should normally go to the store where you bought it. If you don't get satisfaction, write the manufacturer. If you draw a blank there, try writing the state consumer protection agency in the manufacturer's home state (see II-F) or an action line there (II-T).

Things get trickier when there's a dry cleaner involved. Let's say you send a pair of pants to the cleaner's and it comes back ruined. You march to the cleaner's and ask for enough money to replace it. No dice, says the cleaner; it's the manufacturer's fault. You write to the manufacturer, which says the whole thing was the cleaner's fault. This runaround could go on indefinitely. But there's an organization that can help pin the responsibility where it belongs. That organization is the International Fabricare Institute, 12251 Tech Road, Silver Spring, MD 20904. It can inspect a garment and render an opinion on whether the garment was damaged by inept cleaning or was defective to start with.

But the institute has some rather strict rules. To begin with, it won't accept the garment from you. The garment must be forwarded to the institute by either (1) the dry cleaner, (2) the store that sold you the item, (3) a consumer protection agency, or (4) a Better Business Bureau. What's more, you have to pay an analysis fee ($6 as of early 1980) before the institute will render its opinion.

I suggest you ask the cleaner to forward the garment to the institute, if you get caught in a runaround. If the cleaner refuses, I'd go to the Better Business Bureau. If the garment is worth enough to make payment of the $6 fee sensible, I'd ask the BBB to forward the garment to the institute. If the garment was worth only, say, $15 or less to start with, I'd forget about the institute, but still make a complaint to the BBB. See II-D for addresses of Better Business Bureaus.

Condominiums. The offer looked simply too good to pass up. The condominium unit wasn't too costly. The annual maintenance fees were modest. Financing was available. The condominium was in a resort area, so you figured you could make up a good portion of its cost by renting it out during the tourist season. The prospect of owning your own home, and having a tax shelter (through mortgage interest payments) to boot, appealed to you.

Only, a few troubles cropped up. The maintenance fees, low the first year, have gone up substantially. The developer retained title to the swimming pool, golf course, and parking facilities, and is charging you stiff fees for the use of each. You found out that if you rent your unit out when you go on vacation, you'll have to put a large portion of the income into a pooled fund. The proceeds will be shared by all the unit owners, and the developer will get a cut. And you learned there's nothing in your contract guaranteeing you any compensation if the developer decides to gut the whole place ten years from now and put up a shopping center. It turns out the developer still owns the land.

Well, the troubles described are a conglomerate of extremes. It's unlikely that *all* of them would happen to you. And if you were lucky, or skillful, when you bought your condominium unit, your contract protected you against all of these problems.

If you do have a problem, the best way to solve it is almost certainly by acting in concert with other members of the owners' association at your condominium development. Any problem you have is almost certainly shared by others. Your bargaining power and your ability to afford legal advice or the costs of any necessary litigation will be much greater if you're acting together than if you're acting separately. In addition to seeking legal advice, you and the other owners should draft a letter to your state consumer-protection agency (see II-F), and to the Federal Trade Commission (II-H). Don't overlook city and county agencies (II-E): They may be crucial to your struggle. In recent years, a number of municipalities and counties have passed condominium ordinances. The overall trend is to increase the rights of unit owners and to limit the ability of developers to hold long-term leases and milk the unit owners for every last drop of profit.

Contests. The letter always seems to be written in bold type. "Good news for the [your name filled in by typewriter] family," it may begin. "You have won a valuable prize!"

Often, all you've won is the "right" to buy something from the company whose "contest" you've just "won."

Sometimes they make you work for your "prize" by doing something hard, like telling how many states there are in the United States.

In short, some contests are simply sales gimmicks. Much of the time such ploys are merely annoying. (Personally, I throw all such "good news" in the garbage.) However, you may enter a contest in good faith and then find there are strings attached to your victory. If the contest was designed to mislead you, you may well have a valid complaint of fraud or unfair sales practices. Report it to your state consumer protection agency (II-F) and also, if they're distinct, your state attorney general's office. Also report it to the Better Business Bureau (II-D).

If the contest is local, you should report any unfair shenanigans to your city or county consumer agency (II-E), if you have one. If it's an interstate contest, you should also complain to the consumer agency in the sponsor's home state (see II-F again). Finally, if the contest is run by mail, and you believe it was run unfairly or deceptively, report the facts to the Postal Inspector in Charge at the nearest large post office. (Your local post office can tell you the address.)

Contractors. See Home Improvements and Repairs.

Correspondence Schools. See Vocational Schools.

Cosmetics. If there's a fly in your ointment, direct your complaint to the Food and Drug Administration (see II-I). The FDA is responsible for seeing that cosmetics are pure. It's also responsible for seeing that as few people as possible suffer allergic reactions to them. If you experience such a reaction, by all means report it. That will help the FDA better police the cosmetics marketplace.

You may want to send a copy of your correspondence

with the FDA to the manufacturer, if you write the company to request a refund.

If you have a complaint about a personal care product, but you're not sure the product counts as a cosmetic, direct your complaint to the FDA anyway. The product probably *is* a cosmetic, under the definition used in the FDA's enabling statute. This definition includes not only such items as perfume, lipstick, and eye shadow, but also such things as toothpaste, hair dye, and soap—pretty much any chemical composition that you can apply in any way to your body.

If your problem with a cosmetic concerns its failure to get the right person to fall into your arms, direct your complaint —subtly—to that person.

Credit Problems. (See also Billing; Debt Collection; Discrimination.) We'll discuss here three major types of problems you might have: (1) being turned down for a loan; (2) being deceived in connection with a loan; or (3) being billed for defective goods or services.

(1) *Refusal of credit.* If you're turned down for a loan. you have a legal right to know why. In particular, you have a right to know if the company that refused you the loan obtained a report on you from a credit bureau. (Such reports constitute what people think of as their "credit rating.") Credit bureaus are private firms that make money by collecting information on people and passing it on to banks, loan companies, insurance companies, and employers. They may also share information with each other. The largest credit bureaus maintain extraordinarily extensive files: Equifax, for example, prepares some 34 million credit reports on individuals each year.

If a credit bureau's report was a factor in a decision to deny you a loan, the bank or loan company must tell you so. It must also give you the name and address of the bureau where it got the report. You can then contact the credit bureau and find out what's being said about you. Under current law, you're not entitled to see your file. Rather, an employee of the credit bureau reads you what's in it, leaving out the names of any confidential informants the bureau used to gather its information.

If you think the information in your file is wrong, say so. Say so in person, then go home and say so in writing, in a letter to the credit bureau, with a copy to the place that refused you the loan. Under the Fair Credit Reporting Act, the bureau must reinvestigate your situation.

But suppose the bureau reinvestigates and still says it's correct? Then you have the right to have your own written version of the facts placed in your file. The credit bureau must give your statement, along with its own report, to anyone who asks for information on you in the future.

If you have a complaint about a credit bureau, the best place to take it is probably the Federal Trade Commission. You can phone or write an FTC local office (see II-H), or you can write to the Director, Division of Credit Practices, Federal Trade Commission, Washington DC 20580. You may also want to try your state consumer protection agency (II-F).

If you think you've been turned down for a loan because of discrimination (on grounds of race, sex, marital status, national origin, or religion), file a complaint with the appropriate banking authority (see Banks) and with the authorities listed under Discrimination.

(2) *Deceptive lending practices.* Not getting a loan is one thing. Getting one is something else again—and it, too, can be a problem. The interest rate, the provisions for early or late payment, and other terms of the loan will normally be spelled out in the loan contract. But these terms can be hard to understand, and may sometimes be misrepresented by a

lender. The Truth in Lending Act requires that loan terms be accurately spelled out in writing and that the interest rate always be expressed as an annual percentage rate (APR).

One abuse you may encounter in connection with a loan is the lender's insistence that you carry credit insurance. This is a mini-insurance policy that makes sure the debt would be paid off if you died (or, with some policies, if you were disabled). Lenders like it for several reasons. First, it reduces their bad debt costs. Second, they get a fat commission (from the insurance company) for selling it. Third, they make money by lumping the premium for the insurance in with the loan, and charging you interest on the whole thing. If you already have a decent amount of insurance, there's probably no reason why you should pay extra to insure each debt you may have. What's more, credit insurance tends to be expensive (per $1,000 of coverage) compared to conventional life insurance. Some lenders may try to give you the impression that credit insurance is required. That's hardly ever the case. Under the Truth in Lending Act, credit insurance can be required *only* if its cost is included in the APR. Lenders don't usually wish to do this, especially if their APR is already as high as state law permits. So credit insurance is for all practical purposes voluntary. If someone tells you otherwise, he may well be deceiving you.

If you feel that you've been deceived in any way in connection with a loan, your best recourse will usually be a banking agency (see Banks), the FTC (see II-H), or a special state office that regulates credit practices, if your state has one. You might also want to try your state consumer protection agency (II-F), or a city or county agency (II-E).

(3) *Billing for defective goods or services.* A different type of credit problem arises when you're billed for defective goods or services. What you do depends on whether the bill

comes from the seller or from a third party, like Master Card or Visa.

If the bill comes from the company that sold you the defective item or job, your best bet is usually to pay only the part of the bill you think is legitimate. Accompany your partial payment with a letter (of which you keep a photocopy). In the letter, spell out exactly what the seller did wrong, and what he would have to do (such as a replacement or repair) to get the rest of the money. If you can't conceive of any circumstance in which you would pay the disputed amount, be forthright and say so. Keep your copy of the letter and other documents related to the dispute together in a convenient place. Read the entry under Debt Collection so you'll know your rights in the event the seller starts collection proceedings against you. If you think you're likely to wind up in court, consult a lawyer, but this step isn't necessary for routine disputes.

Remember, you always have available the alternate strategy of paying the whole bill and then going to small claims court to sue the seller. Usually, though, this is second best. You're better off having the money in your own hands: This gives you some leverage and bargaining power. So long as you hold the money, *they* have to sue *you* to get it. And, if you're in the right, they're not too likely to do so, though they may threaten.

Now let's look at the case where the bill comes not directly from the seller but rather from a third party. The third party may be a general purpose credit card company (e.g., American Express, Master Card, Visa, or the like) or a finance company, to whom some vendor sold your installment contract. (When you buy a car, an appliance, or furniture on an installment basis, the seller may sell the right to receive your payments to a finance company. In return, the seller gets a slightly reduced lump sum, but doesn't have to worry about collecting payments.) The question in your mind is, "Why should the credit card company or the finance company care about my dispute? It doesn't directly involve them, after all."

In years past, the answer was often that the third party *didn't* give a hoot about your dispute. It just collected your money. If what you bought for that money was defective, you could complain to the original seller. But the original seller, having already gotten paid by the third party, couldn't care less about your problem.

This legalized runaround, so frustrating to consumers, was called the "holder in due course" doctrine. It held that when the holder of an IOU (a debt) passed that collectible debt on to a third party (the holder in due course), the new holder had a right to collect, regardless of any disputes surrounding the original transaction.

You might still encounter this doctrine. You might even have unwittingly agreed to it, in the fine print of a loan or installment contract. But it doesn't matter. The doctrine is dead. Under an FTC ruling ("Preservation of Consumers' Claims and Defenses") made in 1976, the third party is no longer entitled to collect your money, no matter what. You can tell the third party that the goods or services were defective. If the third party sues you, you can use the defectiveness issue as a valid defense in court. In short, there's no longer any legal way in which you can be compelled to pay for defective goods.

Incidentally, this new rule makes it more important than ever for you to keep copies of complaint letters you send regarding defects on any major purchases.

If the third party in one of these triangles happens to be a bank credit card company or a general purpose credit card company, your rights are even clearer. Under the Fair Credit Billing Act, you may send a letter to the card issuer explaining why you're paying only part (or none) of the bill. The card issuer then has three choices. It can swallow the loss. It can get involved in mediating the dispute. Or it can return the debt to the store to collect. (Card issuers will usually choose the third option.)

Technically, your rights under the Fair Credit Billing Act apply only to purchases involving $50 or more, and made within one hundred miles of your home. In practice, you should probably attempt to ignore these restrictions, at least for as long as possible. The spirit behind the legislation is to turn the credit card issuer into an active force for resolving the dispute. If you pay up without a fight, you've forfeited a lot of your leverage.

If you have a problem involving the holder-in-due-course doctrine or the Fair Credit Billing Act, your recourses may include the FTC (see II-H); the appropriate banking agency, if a bank card's involved (see Banks); your specialized state credit agency, if any, and your state consumer protection agency (see II-F).

Credit Unions. See Banks.

Dating Services. If the dating service introduces you only to sex maniacs (or, depending on your preferences, fails to introduce you to any sex maniacs), your rights in the situation are usually determined by what the service promised in its contract with you, or in its advertising. Your logical recourses here are usually county or city consumer agencies (II-E), state consumer protection agencies (II-F), or the local Better Business Bureau (II-D).

Debt Collection. (See also Billing; Credit Problems.) If

someone's trying to collect money from you that you don't believe you really owe, you'll find advice under Billing or

Credit Problems. If you do indeed owe it and just can't pay it, this passage is intended for you.

There are basically four ways a creditor can seek to collect a debt from you: through threats, through a lawsuit, through garnishment, and through repossession. If the business to which you owe money is legitimate, the only threat it can make is use of the other three methods.

If the business is not legitimate—if, for example, you made the mistake of borrowing money from a loan shark—your recourse agency is the police. You should go to them as quickly and as discreetly as possible.

If a bill collector uses threats, harassment tactics, or abusive language, contact the Federal Trade Commission (II-H), your state consumer protection agency (II-F), your state attorney general's office (if it's distinct from the consumer agency), and your local consumer protection agency, if you have one (see II-E).

If a bill collector calls so repeatedly on the telephone as to constitute harassment, or if he calls at late hours, complain to the Federal Trade Commission (II–H) and to the telephone company. Such practices are illegal under the rules of the Federal Communications Commission. The FCC has delegated to the phone companies the task of taking action against collectors who use those kinds of harassment tactics. (If the phone company refuses to help, you may wish to complain about the phone company to your public utilities commission—see list of these under Utilities and Utility Bills.)

If a bill collector sends you what purports to be a court form (but isn't), or if a bill collector impersonates a government agency, notify the Federal Trade Commission (II-H) and your state consumer protection agency (II-F). Such practices are clearly fraudulent; they're forbidden by statute in many states and by common law in others.

Under the Fair Debt Collection Practices Act of 1978, any

debt collector who calls you must furnish you (within five days of the call) a written statement of exactly how much you owe, to whom, and what you can do if you believe the bill is in error. Collection agencies can't phone you at work, unless it's okay with you and with your employer. Nor can collection agencies try to shame you by contacting your friends or neighbors. The Federal Trade Commission (II-H) is responsible for enforcing the Fair Debt Collection Practices Act. You should also report violations to your state consumer protection agency (II-F).

So far we've been talking about things bill collectors can't legally do. Now let's talk about the things they *can* do—lawsuits, garnishment, and repossession.

The best way to stave off a lawsuit is to pay as much as you can, *regularly,* and to communicate honestly with your creditors in writing about your difficulty in paying their bills. If you do this, they may threaten to sue you, but they're unlikely actually to do so. If you are sued, your creditor can win a court judgment forcing you to pay up. If that happens, you may have to sell your assets, such as a house, car, or furniture, in order to meet the debt. Or, alternatively, you could declare bankruptcy.

Declaring bankruptcy is not the end of the world. It is a legal proceeding—a fairly simple one, in many states—under which you pay what you can to your creditors and are released from what then remains of your debts. The advantage is that you'll be free of your debts. A disadvantage is that your credit rating will probably carry the record of the bankruptcy for at least fourteen years. During this time you will find it difficult if not impossible to get credit cards or loans. You may also have difficulty in obtaining insurance, or in getting a new job.

These are real drawbacks, but bankruptcy can also have real advantages for some individuals. Not only are your debts canceled, allowing you to make a fresh start, but you are allowed to keep certain minimum items to make that fresh start possible. What are those items? It depends on what state you live in. However, there is a standard list of property you get to keep, contained in the federal bankruptcy law, as revised in 1979. The list includes (1) tools of your trade, up to $750; (2) equity in a house (or, ironically enough, a burial plot) up to $7,500; (3) equity in a car or truck, up to $1,200; (4) prescription drugs or medical devices, with no fixed maximum limit; (5) jewelry, up to $500; (6) miscellaneous personal property, up to $400. If you didn't use up the $7,500 exemption for home equity, it can be applied to your miscellaneous personal property. This summary of the list is not intended to be complete. If you are contemplating bankruptcy, you can get an updated and more complete version of the list from a lawyer.

Whether the standard list applies to you or not depends on where you live. Congress provided the federal bankruptcy law to be available as an option unless a state legislature specifically rejects it. Florida and Virginia have rejected it, and other states are considering doing so. In those states, if you go bankrupt, the list of property you're allowed to keep may be considerably shorter. On the other hand, there are some states that may allow you to keep *more* property than you would under the standard federal list. The federal law ordinarily lets you choose either the federal or the state terms. If you live in one of these more generous states, naturally you'd use your state's terms.

Before you even consider bankruptcy, you should understand that there are some types of debts it can't wipe out. These include most debts owed to the government (e.g., taxes and fines), as well as alimony and child support. Also, in many cases, so-called secured debts have to be paid. These are debts in which you've put up property as collateral for a loan. The classic example is a home mortgage, in which the bank can foreclose and take title to the house if you don't make your payments.

If you ever find yourself considering bankruptcy, you may also want to consider the alternative of a Chapter 13 proceeding. (Straight bankruptcy is a Chapter 7 proceeding.) Chapter 13 is for people who believe they can repay all or a substantial part of their debts, given additional time. It involves drawing up a repayment plan under which debts are repaid over a period of time—usually three years. Once a court has approved a Chapter 13 plan, your creditors can't hound you for the whole total due them, but must accept gradual repayment. The advantages of the plan are that it doesn't require you to surrender your assets, it may be gentler on your credit rating, and it may make you feel better about yourself. The chief disadvantage, as expressed by consumer advocate Herb Denenberg, is that it may just "prolong the agony."

Bankruptcy is also a potential shield against the other two tactics in the bill collector's repertoire, garnishment and repossession. But it's not the only shield against these tactics.

Garnishment, sometimes called wage attachment, is a process in which a creditor goes to your employer and demands to be paid a slice out of your salary before you are. This tactic is legal, but there's a limit on how big a slice can be taken. Under federal law, a creditor can't take more than a quarter of your after-tax earnings. Nor can a creditor take so much that you're left with less than thirty times the hourly U.S. minimum wage as your weekly take-home pay. Some state laws offer you further protection in regard to the size of the creditor's slice. So, if you discover that your wages have been attached, telephone your state consumer protection agency (II-F) to find out what your rights are.

Repossession, as its name implies, is a process in which a

company that sold you something takes it back because you've fallen behind in your payments. This, too, is legal. In most states it's legal even without any warning to you. (Many a debtor has awakened in the morning to find that his car has been jump-started during the night and driven away by a "repo man" working for a creditor.)

If something of yours is repossessed, you would be wise *immediately* to contact your state consumer protection agency (see II-F) and your city or county consumer agency, if any (see II-E), to find out your rights. You probably should also contact a lawyer. I know a lawyer is the last thing you think you can afford when you're in debt, but a good lawyer can often be of great help in dealing with matters of bankruptcy or repossession. Discuss fees frankly at the outset. In some cases, you may be able to get excellent advice from a Legal Aid lawyer, whose services are paid for out of public funds.

Though creditors in most states don't have to warn you before they repossess something, they *do* have to tell you how, when, and where they plan to sell it again. In some states you can try to buy the item back, in others not. (Do you begin to see why I say you should consult a lawyer?) But whether or not you're allowed to bid, you should try to be present when the item is sold, or at least keep close tabs on what happens to it. Many merchants will strike up a deal with somebody and sell the merchandise at an artificially low price. Then you're out your merchandise and may still owe the merchant the difference between what he resold the item for and what you owed him on it when it was repossessed.

Suppose you bought a $3,000 car, paid $1,000 on it in monthly installments, and then fell behind. The merchant could repossess the car, sell it for $500 (perhaps getting more under the table), and still claim that you owed him $1,500. You could be out both the merchandise and the money. Note, though, that in some enlightened states the merchant can have either your money or his goods back, but not both. Because the laws vary from state to state, and because some states are in the process of reforming their laws, it's imperative that you get quick, sound advice. That's why you may do best to contact both a state agency and a lawyer.

If repossessed goods are sold for *more* than you owed—if, for example, that car was resold for $2,100—then the merchant who repossessed your goods owes *you* money. Few debtors collect this money, mostly because they don't know they have it coming. You know, however. And that knowledge could enable you to eke a small consolation payment out of your financial setback.

Deceptive Advertising. See Advertising.

Dehumidifiers. See Appliances and Appliance Repairs.

Delivery of Merchandise. (See also Mail-Order Houses.) The store told you your new furniture (washing machine, patio blocks, whatever) would be delivered in two weeks. Now it's been five and a half weeks; still no sign of it. When you call the store to complain, you're told your merchandise should be in shortly. There was a little problem at the supplier's end.

What do you do? It depends on how much you want this particular merchandise, and on whether anyone else carries it. If this store is the only one that has the very item you want, you have to grit your teeth and wait. Meanwhile, you can file a complaint with the Better Business Bureau (see II-D) to warn other consumers.

If you can find the same item available off the shelf at another store, or if you decide to settle for a comparable item, you can cancel your original order. The store may give you a fuss about this. If they won't accept your cancellation, you can turn for help to a state or local consumer protection agency (II-F and II-E), to a voluntary consumer group (II-Q), or to a media action line (II-T). Cancellation works best as a strategy when you haven't already paid for the goods. If you've already paid, you may need to go to small claims court (II-N) to get your money back. Of course, you're on much stronger ground in canceling an order (or demanding a speedup of delivery) if you have a written commitment on the delivery date. For this reason, always try to have the delivery date written on the sales slip.

At least one state, Rhode Island, has a law providing that you're entitled to cancellation of your order—and a full refund—if a store is more than thirty days late in delivering something. In lieu of a refund, you may select a comparable item, or a credit against future purchases. I haven't found any nationwide rundown to determine whether other states have legislation comparable to Rhode Island's. You can find out from your state consumer protection agency (II-F).

Discrimination. Few hassles you encounter in daily life are as discouraging—and infuriating—as discrimination. If someone turns you down for something (be it a loan, insurance, a job, or whatever) or otherwise mistreats you because of your race, sex, or age, you have every reason to be furious. You also, fortunately, have a number of places you can turn for help.

One useful resource, especially if race is an issue, is the U.S. Commission on Civil Rights, 1121 Vermont Ave. NW, Washington DC 20425. It's not likely that the commission would be able to handle your complaint directly, but it may well have a good idea where to refer it.

Discrimination complaints are one type of complaint that you may well want to take to your elected representatives, on the local, state, or federal level. Your city council representative, your state senator or representative, or a U.S. senator or representative may take an interest in your problem. To put it bluntly, there's a certain amount of political advantage in helping people out with discrimination problems.

Don't overlook local chapters of such national groups as American Civil Liberties Union (ACLU), National Association for the Advancement of Colored People (NAACP), National Organization for Women (NOW), or the Grey Panthers. The quality of the help you get from your local chapter of such a group can vary from nil to invaluable. They're worth trying, since in some cases the staffers know the way to get things done within the local power structure, have handled similar complaints before, and are eager to help.

Most states have a civil rights agency. Addresses for these agencies are listed at the end of this section.

Other potential sources of help may be available for discrimination problems in particular areas. Let's look in turn at discrimination in banking or credit, in employment or hiring, in housing, and in education.

If your problem concerns banking or credit, read the entries in this book under Banks and Credit Problems to get specific ideas of where to go for help. The Fair Credit Opportunity Act specifically forbids any lender or issuer of credit to discriminate against anyone because of race, color, age, sex, marital status, religion, or receipt of public assistance.

If your problem concerns hiring or employment practices, the local office of the U.S. Department of Labor is one resource you might try. Another is the Equal Employment Opportunity Commission (EEOC), Washington DC 20506.

However, these two federal agencies usually move slowly, if at all, in response to individual complaints. They are likely to take action only when they receive several complaints against a particular employer. So go ahead and file your complaints with the federal agencies, but simultaneously consider action on other fronts. Write or phone your state civil rights agency (listed below). Consult with an attorney to consider a lawsuit or the threat of a lawsuit. If you can't afford an attorney, find out whether you're eligible for a Legal Aid attorney. (Your county government information officers should be able to answer this question.)

If you feel you've been discriminated against in housing, you may be able to get redress under the terms of the Civil Rights Act of 1968. As interpreted by the Department of Housing and Urban Development (HUD), the act bans (1) steering—the process by which a real estate person might try to get you to buy or rent in a specific neighborhood or building, based on your race, color, age, sex, religion, or origin; (2) redlining—a situation in which lending institutions refuse to write mortgages in a particular area of a city or region; and (3) sales discrimination—the refusal to sell to you because of any of the factors mentioned above (race, religion, etc.). If you believe you've suffered from one of these forms of housing discrimination, write Director, Fair Housing and Equal Opportunity, Department of Housing and Urban Development, Washington DC 20410. Or call, toll-free, 800-424-8590. (The toll free number's not good in the District of Columbia; if you're a DC resident, phone 755-7252.) Also contact your state civil rights agency. Don't overlook the citizens' groups mentioned earlier. And don't hesitate to contact one of your political representatives.

If you feel you've been discriminated against by an educational institution, contact your political representatives and the state civil rights agency. Also send a copy of your complaint to the Office of Civil Rights, Department of Education, Washington, DC 20201.

Here are the addresses of the state civil rights agencies and/or fair employment agencies in states and the District of Columbia. So far as I know, no such state offices exist in Alabama, Louisiana, Mississippi, or Texas. (Federal officials or legal actions may offer your best hope in these states.)

Alaska

- Human Rights Commission, Office of the Governor, 204 E. Fifth Ave., Room 213, Anchorage, AK 99501
- Equal Employment Opportunity Officer, Division of Administrative Services, Dept. of Health & Social Services, Pouch H-02, Juneau, AK 99811

Arizona

- Civil Rights Division, Dept. of Law, 1700 W. Washington, Phoenix, AZ 85007

Arkansas

- Manager, Division of Community Services, Dept. of Local Services, #1 Capitol Mall, Little Rock, AR 72201
- Director of Equal Employment Opportunity, Employment Security Division, Dept. of Labor, ESD Building, Capitol Mall, Little Rock, AR 72201

California

- Division of Fair Employment Practices, Dept. of Industrial Relations, PO Box 603, San Francisco, CA 94101

Colorado

- Civil Rights Division, Dept. of Regulatory Agencies, 600 State Services Building, 1525 Sherman St., Denver, CO 80203

Connecticut

- Commission on Human Rights and Opportunities, 90 Washington St., Hartford, CT 06115

Delaware

- Office of Human Relations, Dept. of Community Affairs and Economic Development, Williams State Service Center, 805 River Road, Dover, DE 19901
- Dept. of Labor, Delaware State Building, 820 French St., Wilmington, DE 19801

District of Columbia

- Office of Human Rights, Executive Office of the Mayor, 1329 E Street NW, Washington DC 20004

Florida

- Commission on Human Relations, 2571 Executive Center Circle, East, Tallahassee, FL 32301
- Office of Civil Rights, Dept. of Labor and Employment Security, Berkeley Building, Tallahassee, FL 32301

Georgia

- Special Assistant to the Govenor for Civil Rights, Office of the Governor, Room 245, State Capitol, Atlanta, GA 30334
- Office of Fair Employment Practices, Room 685, 254 Washington St., Atlanta, GA 30334

Hawaii

- Office of Affirmative Action, Office of the Governor, Room 443, State Capitol, Honolulu, HI 96813
- Enforcement Division, Dept. of Labor and Industrial Relations, 825 Mililani St., Honolulu, HI 96813

Idaho

- Human Rights Commission, Office of the Governor, State House, Boise, ID 83720

Illinois

- Commission on Human Relations, Room 1735, 160 N. LaSalle St., Chicago, IL 60601
- Fair Employment Practices Commission, 3 W. Old State Capitol Plaza, Springfield, IL 62701

Indiana

- Civil Rights Commission, Room 319 Fair Building, 311 W. Washington St., Indianapolis, IN 46204
- Affirmative Action Section, State Personnel Division, 507 State Office Building, Indianapolis, IN 46204

Iowa

- Civil Rights Commission, 418 Sixth St., Des Moines, IA 50319

Kansas

- Commission on Civil Rights, 535 Kansas Ave., Topeka, KS 66603
- Equal Employment Opportunity Office, Dept. of Administration, Room 542, 503 Kansas Ave., Topeka, KS 66603

Kentucky

- Commission on Human Rights, Capital Plaza Tower, Frankfort, KY 40601
- Coordinator, External (or Internal) Equal Employment Opportunity, Dept. of Personnel, Capitol Annex, Frankfort, KY 40601

Maine

- Human Rights Commission, State House, Augusta, ME 04333

Maryland

- Human Relations Commission, Metro Plaza at Mondawmin Mall, #300, Baltimore, MD 21215

Massachusetts

- Commission Against Discrimination, Executive Office for Administration and Planning, 1 Ashburton Place, Boston, MA 02108
- Director, Affirmative Action, 1 Ashburton Place, Boston, MA 02108

Michigan

- Dept. of Civil Rights, 10th Floor, 125 W. Allegan, Lansing, MI 48913

Minnesota

- Dept. of Human Rights, 240 Bremer Building, 419 N. Robert St., St. Paul, MN 55101

Missouri

- Commission on Human Rights, Dept. of Consumer Affairs, Regulation and Licensing, 204 Metro, PO Box 1129, Jefferson City, MO 65101

Montana

- Human Rights Division, Dept. of Labor and Industry, Room 404, 7 W. Sixth Ave., Helena, MT 59601
- Equal Employment Opportunity Supervisor, Dept. of Administration, Room 101, Mitchell Building, Helena, MT 59601

Nebraska

- Equal Opportunity Commission, 301 Centennial Mall, S., Lincoln, NB 68509

Nevada

- Equal Rights Commission, 1515 E. Tropicana Blvd., #590, Las Vegas, NV 89590

New Hampshire

- Commission for Human Rights, 61 S. Spring St., Concord, NH 03301

New Jersey

- Division of Civil Rights, Dept. of Law and Public Safety, 1100 Raymond Blvd., Newark, NJ 07102

New Mexico

- Human Rights Commission, 303 Bataan Memorial Building, Santa Fe, NM 87503

New York

- Division of Human Rights, Executive Dept., 53d Floor, 2 World Trade Center, New York, NY 10047

North Carolina

- Human Relations Council, Dept. of Administration, 530 N. Wilmington St., Raleigh, NC 27604

North Dakota

- Labor Dept., 5th Floor, State Capitol, Bismarck, ND 58505

Ohio

- Civil Rights Commission, 220 Parsons Ave., Columbus, OH 43215

Oklahoma

- Human Rights Commission, G-11 Jim Thorpe Building, Oklahoma City, OK 73105

Oregon

- Civil Rights Division, Bureau of Labor, State Office Building, 4th Floor, Portland, OR 97201
- Employment Division, Dept. of Human Resources, 875 Union St. NE, Salem, OR 97310

Pennsylvania

- Human Relations Commission, Office of the Governor, 100 N. Cameron St., Harrisburg, PA 17101

Rhode Island

- Commission for Human Rights, 334 Westminster Mall, Providence, RI 02903

South Carolina

- Human Affairs Commission, PO Box 11300, Columbia, SC 29211

South Dakota

- Division of Human Rights, Dept. of Commerce and Consumer Affairs, State Capitol, Pierre, SD 57501

- State Equal Employment Opportunity Officer, Bureau of Personnel, Dept. of Executive Management, State Capitol, Pierre, SD 57501

Tennessee

- Commission for Human Development, C3-305 Cordell Hull Building, Nashville, TN 37219
- Division of Equal Opportunity, Dept. of Employment Security, 529 Cordell Hull Building, Nashville, TN 37219

Utah

- Antidiscrimination Division, Industrial Commission, 350 E. 500 South St., Salt Lake City, UT 84111
- Dept. of Employment Security, Industrial Commission, PO Box 11249, Salt Lake City, UT 84147

Vermont

- Civil Rights Division, Office of Attorney General, Pavilion Office Building, 109 State St., Montpelier, VT 05602

Virginia

- Equal Opportunity and Employee Programs, Dept. of Personnel and Training, State Finance Building, Richmond, VA 23219

Washington

- Human Rights Commission, 402 Evergreen Plaza Building, Olympia, WA 98504

West Virginia

- Human Rights Commission, 402 Evergreen Plaza Build-1036 Quarrier St., Charleston, WV 25301
- Affirmative Action Officer, Governor's Office, WR-9 State Capitol, Charleston, WV 25305

Wisconsin

- Equal Rights Division, Dept. of Industry, Labor and Human Relations, 201 E. Washington Ave., Madison, WI 53702

Wyoming

- Attorney General, 123 State Capitol, Cheyenne, WY 82002
- Dept. of Labor and Statistics, Barrett Building, Cheyenne, WY 82002

Dishwashers. See Appliances and Appliance Repairs.

Distributorships. Being a distributor for a product is fine. Being a dupe of a phony distribution scheme isn't. There are certain danger signs that can help you distinguish a legitimate distributorship from a pyramid scheme. If a legitimate firm tries to recruit you as a distributor, it won't promise you instant riches. It will probably offer to buy back from you any goods that you can't sell, at something like 90 percent of the price you paid for them. It will not charge you a large initial investment fee. Most of all, it will emphasize selling the product, not recruiting subdistributors.

The hallmark of a pyramid scheme is that you're supposed to make money by recruiting subdistributors into the scheme. In this regard, it resembles nothing so much as an old-fashioned chain letter. Chain letters are widely illegal, and so are pyramid schemes, for the same reason: There aren't enough potential recruits in the world to make either kind of scheme profitable for anyone except those who get in early in the game. Those who come in later are bound to lose; their money winds up in the pockets of the earlybirds who win. That "win," however, could end in a conviction, as more and more states outlaw pyramid plans.

If you've been duped by a pyramid plan masquerading as a distributorship, or if someone suggests you become involved in one, report it to your state consumer protection agency (see II-F) and also (if they're distinct) to your state attorney general's office. If use of the mails is involved, be sure to contact the Inspection Service of the U.S. Postal Service. You can do this through your local postmaster, through your local postal inspector, or by writing the Chief Postal Inspector, U.S. Postal Service, Room 3517, Washington DC 20260.

Doctors and Dentists. See Medical Treatment.

Door-to-Door Sales. Door-to-door salespeople are (a) honest, hardworking people; (b) crooks; (c) decent people who may tend to exaggerate at times the merits of their wares. Which would you check? Whatever your pick, you're bound to be wrong at least some of the time. More than two million people sell goods or services door to door. Whatever your preconceived image may be, the reality may be at times better or worse.

If you give in to a persuasive pitch and regret it later, you can take advantage of a three-day cooling-off period. A Federal Trade Commission (FTC) regulation gives you three business days to cancel a purchase. The regulation applies only to purchases of $25 or more, and it applies only to genuine door-to-door sales—in other words, not to cases where you've *asked* a salesperson to come to your home.

The salesperson, under the regulation, is required to provide you at the time of sale with a "notice of cancellation" that you can send in if you change your mind within the three days. Legally, all you have to do to cancel the sale is to fill out this notice and mail it (by regular mail) before the time limit expires. Personally, I recommend going a bit beyond these legal requirements. I think you should make a photocopy of the filled-in cancellation notice, and I think you should send the notice by certified mail, return receipt requested. (This is easily done and not expensive; your local post office can help you.)

When the seller receives a cancellation notice, it must cancel the sale and promptly refund any money you've paid. Failure to do so subjects the seller to FTC penalties which can theoretically include a fine up to $10,000.

If you feel your rights under the FTC rule have been violated, you can contact your local FTC office (see II-H), or write to "Cooling Off," Federal Trade Commission, Washington DC 20580.

As I said, the FTC rule applies only to purchases of $25 or more. Some states have their own cooling-off rules, with lower dollar limits. Your state consumer protection agency (see II-F) can help inform you of the law in your state, and help you get your rights under it.

If your state has a cooling-off law, don't hesitate to use both your state recourse agencies and the FTC. That might sound like overkill, but if you've just been talked into buying a $399 vacuum cleaner you didn't need, you can use all the help you can get.

Here are a couple of additional technical points about the FTC's cooling-off regulation. It applies not only to sales made in your home, but also to sales made in certain other locations (other than the seller's place of business), such as rented hotel rooms, or selling "parties" in someone's home. It does *not* apply to the sale of emergency home repairs, securities, real estate, or insurance. (For insurance products, state law usually provides a ten-day cooling-off period, though.)

Once the three-day cooling-off period has passed, you should still complain if you feel the product or service was misrepresented, or that you were otherwise gypped. Write to your state consumer protection agency (II-F), your city or county agency, if any (II-E), and your local Better Business Bureau (II-D). Send a copy of your complaint to the Direct

Selling Association, Suite 610, 1730 M Street SW, Washington DC 20036.

Draperies. See Furniture.

Drugs. All complaints concerning drugs should go to the Food and Drug Administration. The FDA's headquarters address is Consumer Communications, HFJ-10, Food and Drug Administration, 5600 Fishers Lane, Rockville, MD 20857. You'll find regional addresses with the discussion of the FDA in section II-I.

If you have an adverse reaction to a drug, report it to your doctor and to the FDA. This will help the FDA do its job, which is to assure that drugs sold in this country are as safe and effective as possible. Don't report to the FDA side effects that you knew in advance (from talking to your doctor or from a package warning label) might occur. But *do* report such side effects to your doctor; he or she might want to change your dosage or change medications.

To avoid problems with drugs, remember that drugs may produce unanticipated or unpleasant effects when they interact. Keep your doctor informed of all drugs you are taking. Remember that over-the-counter drugs (sold without prescription) can be quite potent and that your doctor may not be aware if you're taking one of them. Keep in mind, too, that over-the-counter drugs should never be used for an extended period except on doctor's advice: They can provide just enough relief to mask a serious symptom that should be getting medical attention.

If you have a complaint about a pharmacy, your state board of pharmacy is one place you should take it. (You can usually find this board by looking in state government listings in your capital city phonebook.) Don't stop there, however. State boards of pharmacy are not known as flaming pro-consumer radicals; they have, for example, historically opposed price advertising and even price disclosure. So send copies of your complaint to your city (II-E) and/or state (II-F) consumer protection agencies.

Electric Companies. See Utilities and Utility Bills.

Encyclopedias. To steal a phrase, encyclopedia salesmen "pander to your best instincts." Naturally, you want your kids to have to best in life, to do well in school, to have their souls opened to the wonders of knowledge. But that doesn't necessarily mean you should buy the encyclopedia a salesman is hawking—or any encyclopedia at all if you can't afford it. The bloom of knowledge can be picked in public libraries as well as at home.

Some abuses in the sale of encyclopedias have been reported by the Federal Trade Commission and by *Consumer Reports* magazine. Some of these abuses have been engaged in by sales people for large, reputable encyclopedia publishers. They include (1) the offering of "free" volumes, without adequate disclosure of the strings attached; (2) pressuring people to sign on the spot; (3) implying that a particular encyclopedia is endorsed by a child's school; and (4) representing a commonly used price as a "discount" price.

Since encyclopedias are often sold door to door, the FTC's three-day cooling-off period rule may be helpful here. See the entry on Door-to-Door Sales for a description of the rule. In general, complaints about encyclopedias or unfair tactics used to sell them should be sent to your state consumer protection agency (II-F) and to the Federal Trade Commission (II-H).

Environmental Problems. See Pollution.

False Advertising. See Advertising.

Finance Companies. See Credit Problems; Debt Collection.

Food. (See also Short Weight, Measure, or Count.) If you suspect food is contaminated, wrap it (or what's left of it) in two plastic bags, refrigerate it, and call the appropriate agencies without delay. In many cases, the first agency to call would be your city or county board of health. The board may want to conduct an investigation to see if other food from the same source is contaminated and poses a danger to public health. In some cases, the local board will not have investigative powers and may refer you to the state board of health.

If the contaminated food was meat or poultry, then the U.S. Department of Agriculture (USDA) or your state department of agriculture may come into play. It's not obvious which one to call. If you still have the little blue stamp that tells who inspected the meat, you'll know which agency to contact. If you don't, then you should probably call both state and federal authorities to be on the safe side. However, don't bother with the state department of agriculture if you live in California, Colorado, Connecticut, Kentucky, Massachusetts, Minnesota, Missouri, Montana, Nebraska, Nevada, New Hampshire, New Jersey, New York, North Dakota, Oregon, Pennsylvania, Tennessee, or Washington. In those states all meat and poultry inspection responsibilities have been ceded to the federal government. If a poultry product is involved, don't bother with the state agency in Arkansas, Georgia, Idaho, Maine, Michigan, South Dakota, Utah or West Virginia, either. (Same reason.)

If you encounter contaminated *processed* food (for example, if you find mold in a freshly opened box or can), you should call the nearest office of the Food and Drug Administration (FDA) immediately (see II-I). The FDA has the power to order food-product recalls. Probably the most famous instance of a food recall involved canned vichyssoise that produced a fatal case of botulism poisoning. But the FDA makes large numbers of recalls involving various degrees of urgency. For its supervision of the marketplace to be effective, it depends on citizen complaints.

All right, now you've protected the public health. What about getting your money back? Well, if you inform the store of the problem, possibly passing along a copy of any complaint letter you wrote to the board of health, the agriculture department, or the FDA, the store will probably stumble all over itself in its rush to refund your money. The last thing most food stores need or want is bad publicity. If the store does refuse you a refund, your simplest recourse (assuming very little money's at stake) is just not to shop there again. If you want to fight for a refund, your potential allies include the Better Business Bureau (see II-D), your city or county consumer protection agency, if you have one (II-E), your state consumer agency (II-F), or small claims court (II-N).

What if your problem concerns not the food itself, but the way it was sold? You may feel that a grocery store used deceptive price labels, or advertised specials and then didn't have the items available. (In the latter case, the store may be bound to issue you a rain check, so you can get the sale item later at the sale price. Whether you're entitled to a rain check depends mainly on how the advertisement was worded.) With problems of this sort, your potential recourse agencies are the four mentioned above (II-D, II-E, II-F, and II-N), plus the Federal Trade Commission (II-H), which tries to make sure supermarkets stock adequate supplies of sale items.

Franchises. The best time to get advice regarding a franchise is, of course, before you commit any money to it. You should do a complete research job on both the individual company and the industry it's in. One helpful source of information is the International Franchise Association, Suite 1005, 1025 Connecticut Ave. NW, Washington DC 20036.

Let's say, though, that you're already committed. Now, the franchiser is not giving you the guidance, materials, or financial help it had promised. Or it's failing to give your branch of the franchise as much advertising support as you thought you had coming. Or it's charging you unexpectedly large fees for equipment. What do you do?

Take your problem, and your contract, to a good lawyer. You may want to try to cancel your contract and sue for the return of some or all of your franchise fee. If you decide that's what you want, you can proceed to contact government agencies. Some that may be of help are the nearest office of the federal Small Business Administration (or the SBA's national office at 1441 L Street NW, Washington DC 20416); your state attorney general's office; your state consumer protection agency (see II-F); and the Federal Trade Commission (II-H). Send the franchiser copies of your letters to these agencies.

Alternatively, you may want to pressure the franchiser into providing the promised or needed support. In that case, don't write the government agencies right away. Let your lawyer help you in dealing with the franchiser. Through the threat of a lawsuit and the threat of going to government agencies, you may be able to persuade the franchiser to create a better working relationship.

Fraud. According to the dictionary, fraud is "a deception deliberately practiced in order to secure unfair or unlawful gain." In a sense, much of this book is about fraud and how to combat it. But, legally speaking, most consumer problems stop short of fraud. If someone sells you shoddy goods, you can and should fight to get your money back, or get a replacement or repairs. But fraud isn't involved *unless* the seller knew the goods were shoddy and led you to believe otherwise. To prove fraud, you ordinarily need a written document as evidence of misrepresentation.

To put it another way, if someone does a lousy roofing job on your house, that's a pain in the neck and cause for complaint. If someone puts on lightweight shingles after contracting to install heavyweight ones, that's fraud.

If you're the victim of fraud, you should report it to your state consumer protection agency (see II-F); to your state attorney general's office, if it's distinct from the consumer agency; and, in cases of blatant fraud when you think the perpetrator may be leaving town, to the police.

Freezers. See Appliances and Appliance Repairs.

Fuel Companies. See Utilities and Utility Bills.

Funeral Parlors. Abuses by funeral parlors are widespread. In 1979, the Federal Trade Commission came within a whisker of adopting a rule that would have prohibited certain of the worst practices. A combination of vigorous lobbying by the funeral industry and antiregulatory sentiment on Capitol Hill doomed the rule, at least for the time being. What the FTC had found—and consumer groups had been complaining about for years—was that many funeral parlors were taking advantage of people's grief and vulnerability in a variety of ways. Among the more common:

- Falsely stating that state law requires embalming, a casket, or a burial vault.
- Padding bills for such items as flowers, clergy, or cemetery charges.
- Boycotting or harassing organizations that promote low-cost alternatives to traditional funerals.
- Refusing to quote prices over the telephone.
- Refusing to itemize prices for specific items and services, requiring instead that consumers buy an entire package.
- Playing on people's grief or guilt to make them buy a casket more expensive than they want, need, or can afford.
- Picking up or embalming a body without the family's permission.
- Requiring a casket even if the remains are cremated.

The effect of these practices can add up to a major cash drain on the bereaved's pocketbook. A cremation and simple memorial service can often be something like 75 percent less expensive than a conventional funeral and burial.

If you believe you have been exploited or treated unfairly by a funeral parlor, here are several steps you can take. First, write to the funeral parlor and explain your complaint. If you want money back, ask for a rebate in a specified amount. As with any complaint, keep a photocopy of your letter.

Second, consider bringing your complaint to the attention of your clergyman. He or she may have some leverage, both moral and economic. After all, funeral parlors don't want local clergy to recommend that people go elsewhere.

Third, if you feel you've been victimized by deception or fraud, contact your local Better Business Bureau (see II-D), city or county consumer protection agency (II-E), and state consumer protection agency (II-F).

Fourth, write the FTC (II-H). The FTC has a keen interest in this area. While it may not be able to help with your individual complaint, it can use the information you provide to help regenerate support for its proposed funeral home regulation.

Fifth, consider writing to your elected representatives (II-V). You may want to urge your congressman and senators to support the FTC rule, and cite your experience as an example of the need for it.

By the way, a good source of information on low-cost alternatives to the traditional funeral and burial is the Continental Association of Funeral and Memorial Societies, 1828 Street NW, Washington DC 20036.

Furniture. In 1973, the major furniture manufacturers set up the Furniture Industry Consumer Advisory Panel (FICAP) to handle complaints that can't be resolved between the consumer and the retailer or manufacturer. It mediates disputes informally. If necessary, it also assembles a seven-member panel (consisting of one city consumer protection official, two home economists, a housewife, a home furnishings retailer, a textile expert, and a furniture industry expert) to hear cases in a more formal manner. Judging by press reports I've seen, FICAP (High Point, NC 27260) is doing a good job of handling about four hundred complaints a year. But it seems to be getting only a small fraction of the cases, judging by the large number of complaints about furniture made to state consumer agencies. By all means try FICAP if your complaints to the seller and manufacturer seem to be falling on deaf ears. If FICAP fails, some appropriate next steps would be small claims court (see II-N) or letters to the state consumer protection agencies (II-F) in both your state and the manufacturer's state.

If your problem concerns home furnishings, such as draperies, rather than furniture *per se,* a smaller amount of money may be involved. It may be useful on these complaints to focus on the merchant rather than the manufacturer, using small claims courts or pressing for Better Business Bureau arbitration (II-D). If you wish to bring pressure to bear on the manufacturer, perhaps a letter to the National Curtain, Drapery, and Allied Products Association, 481 Main Street, New Rochelle, NY 10801, would do some good. A letter to the consumer protection agency in the manufacturer's home state again might prove useful here.

Gas Companies. See Utilities and Utility Bills.

Gold. See Precious Metals.

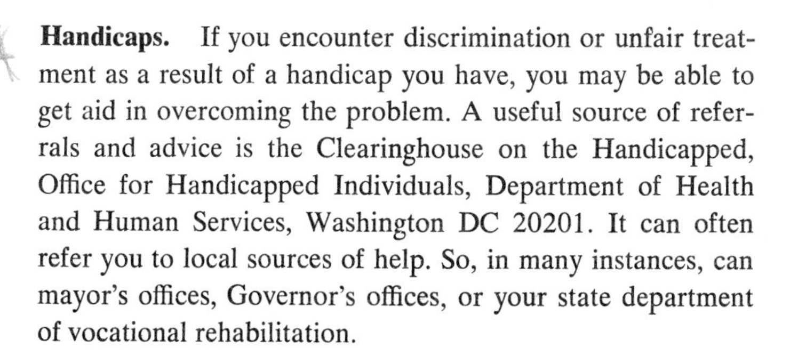

Handicaps. If you encounter discrimination or unfair treatment as a result of a handicap you have, you may be able to get aid in overcoming the problem. A useful source of referrals and advice is the Clearinghouse on the Handicapped, Office for Handicapped Individuals, Department of Health and Human Services, Washington DC 20201. It can often refer you to local sources of help. So, in many instances, can mayor's offices, Governor's offices, or your state department of vocational rehabilitation.

Health Spas. A better body is something most of us would like to have, and a lot of us seek to acquire one by joining a health spa. So far, fine. The problem is that most health spa contracts require you to pay in advance for all, or a large part, of the cost of a series of shape-up sessions. Some spas then keep a very healthy grip on your money, even if you get sick, move away, or decide after one session that exercise isn't your cup of tea after all.

A typical story was told to me by a woman in Chicago: "I enrolled my daughter at a health club, but my daughter changed her mind, as teenagers tend to do. I called the club, and a girl there told me I should just tear up my copy of the contract. Well, because she was so charming, I assumed she was truthful as well. Months later I found they had gotten a judgment against me. And shortly thereafter there was a garnishment against my wages."

In another variation on this theme, new health spas sometimes take large deposits or fees from customers before they even open. Then, sometimes, they never do open, or their opening is repeatedly delayed. Meanwhile, they have the consumer's money and the consumer doesn't.

To remedy this situation, the Federal Trade Commission proposed several years ago a rule that would limit deposits with unopened health spas to 5 percent of the total contract price. The rule would also require all health spas to give pro rata refunds if a customer canceled out without completing the number of sessions specified in the contract. The spa would be allowed to keep no more than 5 percent of the total contract price as a penalty for cancellation. Suppose, for example, that you signed up for ten sessions at a price of $100. If you decided, after the second session, that you didn't care for the spa, you could cancel and be entitled to a refund of $75.

Unfortunately, deliberations on the proposed FTC rule have stretched out for years, and the outlook for passage was uncertain in 1980.

Besides reporting to the FTC (see II-H), you should report complaints about health spas to a Better Business Bureau (II-D), your state consumer protection agency (II-F), and to your city or county consumer agency, if you have one (II-E).

Hearing Aids. For many people a hearing aid can be a blessing. But the way they're advertised and distributed isn't.

Some sellers suggest that a hearing aid is the right solution for any hearing problem. But certain types of problems can't be corrected with a hearing aid. And some overzealous dealers have even gone so far as to try to sell hearing aids to people with normal hearing, according to a 1974 study by a Public Interest Research Group in Queens, New York.

The Federal Trade Commission has also investigated apparent antitrust violations in the hearing aid industry. Several manufacturers allegedly force their distributors to carry one brand only. And exclusive territories are allegedly assigned for dealers, so price competition within brands is virtually eliminated. What's more, dealers are said to be discouraged from offering even replacement parts on other models, so effective servicing of hearing aids is hampered. If you run into any of these problems, call the nearest regional office of the Federal Trade Commission (see II-H).

Under a proposed FTC regulation you would have the right to a thirty-day trial period if you bought a hearing aid. This would go a long way toward curbing the abuses mentioned earlier. If you decided to return the device, you would have to pay a cancellation fee, but it would be only a small fraction of the total cost. The FTC can advise you whether the rule has gone into effect.

Complaints regarding hearing aids should go to the Food and Drug Administration (II-I), as well as to the FTC and your state consumer protection agency (II-F).

Heating. See Home Improvements and Repairs; Utilities and Utility Bills.

Home Furnishings. See Carpeting; Furniture.

Home Improvements and Repairs. This area generates more complaints than any other except automobiles. The phrase "home improvements and repairs" can cover a multitude of sins, and often does! Among the types of work that may be involved are roofing, siding, painting, driveway paving, basement waterproofing, termite inspection or extermination, remodeling, installing swimming pools, and room additions. The number of things that can go wrong is limitless; the ways in which you can be gypped are virtually endless. The vast majority of troubles can be avoided, though, by choosing a reputable, well-established contractor from your local area and by drawing up a complete contract that specifies exactly what is to be done, the exact materials to be used, a completion date, the exact cost, and the time or times when payment is due. The contract should also include protection against mechanic's liens (see below), a provision for cleanup of the work area, and a prohibition against changes in the contract terms unless made in writing and signed by both you and the contractor. Separately, the contractor should give you written assurance that all his workers on the project, whether they're with his own firm or subcontractors, are covered by workmen's compensation insurance.

Of course, if you've already got problems in the home repair or home improvement realm, all of those tips may sound like advising the farmer after his animals have fled through the open barn door. So let's see what we can do about getting the animals back.

To begin with, a few states have laws that require home improvement or repair contractors to give you some of the protections we talked about. In Wisconsin, for example, contractors are legally obligated to provide written contracts before any work is done. In several states contractors are obligated to warn homeowners about mechanic's liens. A mechanic's lien is a judgment (legal claim) against a homeowner's property that can be obtained by a subcontractor or supplier of materials if he isn't paid by the contractor. That means that if you pay your contractor and he goes broke or skips town without paying his subcontractors, you could end up paying for the same work twice. Several states require the contractor to give the homeowner a complete list of all subcontractors and material suppliers. This gives the homeowner a chance to get lien waivers (agreements not to file a mechanic's lien) from them or to demand that the contractor do this. In Wisconsin the contractor is obliged to obtain lien waivers for the homeowner whether the homeowner asks for them or not. Few states are as progressive as Wisconsin in this area, but check with your state consumer protection agency to see what protections you have or had coming to you. If your contractor violated the law, this gives you an extra bargaining chip in trying to get some of your money back from him.

When you communicate with your consumer protection agency, be sure to find out if home improvement and home repair contractors are licensed in your state. If so, get the name and address of the licensing board and file a detailed complaint with it. At the moment this remedy is available in only a minority of states, but the trend seems to be in the direction of more licensing. In some states contractors are required to post a large bond with the state, just in case some abused consumer has to be compensated someday. You might be that consumer.

Another possible source of help is a trade association. The ones listed below are affiliated with the National Home Improvement Council, whose headquarters are at 11 E. 44th St., New York, NY 10017. They vary considerably in how far they can or will go in mediating complaints. But at the least they're an avenue worth checking. (You can also write to the National Home Improvement Council to find out if any new affiliates have sprung up recently in your area.)

The NHIC affiliates as of 1979, listed by state, were: *In*

Alabama, the Home Improvement Council of Birmingham; *in Arkansas,* the National Home Improvement Council of Arkansas (North Little Rock); *in California,* the American Building Contractors Association (Alameda, Los Angeles, Monterey, North Tahoe, Orange County, San Diego, San Francisco, San Gabriel, and Visalia); *in Colorado,* the Home Improvement Association of Metro Denver; *in District of Columbia,* the Washington DC Chapter, NHIC; *in Florida,* the South Florida Chapter of NHIC (North Miami Beach); *in Illinois,* the Professional Remodelers Association of Greater Chicago, and the Central Illinois Home Improvement Association (East Peoria); *in Indiana,* the Greater Fort Wayne Chapter of NHIC; *in Iowa,* the Iowa Chapter of NHIC (Des Moines); *in Maryland,* the Maryland Chapter of NHIC (Towson); *in Massachusetts,* the Eastern Massachusetts Chapter of NHIC (Belmont), and the Western Massachusetts Home Improvement Council (East Longmeadow); *in Minnesota,* the Twin Cities Chapter of NHIC (Minneapolis); *in Michigan,* the Home Improvement Council of Metropolitan Detroit, and the NHIC of Western Michigan (Grand Rapids); *in Missouri,* the Greater Kansas City Home Improvement Contractors' Association, and the Remodeling Guild of Greater St. Louis; *in New York,* the Home Improvement Industry Council (Buffalo), and the New York Chapter of NHIC (Bay Shore); *in Ohio,* the Home Improvement Council of Stark County (Canton), the Home Improvement Council of Greater Cincinnati, the Cleveland Home Improvement Council, and the NHIC of Toledo; *in Oregon,* the Oregon Remodelers Association (Portland); *in Pennsylvania,* the Home Improvement Council of Greater Erie, and the Western Pennsylvania Chapter of NHIC (Pittsburgh); *in South Carolina,* the Home Improvement Council of Greater Columbia; *in Texas,* the National Home Improvement Council of the Greater Metroplex

(Irving); and the Houston Home Improvement Council; *in Utah,* the Utah Home Improvement Council (Salt Lake City); *in Washington,* the Washington Home Improvement Council (Seattle); *in Wisconsin,* the Home Improvement Council of Greater Milwaukee.

If informal mediation through a trade association isn't available or doesn't help, you may want to seek a more formal kind of arbitration. The contractor may refuse to go before a Better Business Bureau panel of arbitrators. But if he's willing, you may save a lot of time and money (in litigation costs) by taking this route (see II-D). Your last resort, assuming that by now you've already filed complaints with your state consumer agency (II-F) and any licensing agency your state has, is to go to court. The amount involved will probably exceed the limit of small claims court jurisdiction, so you'll need a lawyer (see II-O). But his fee may be well spent if it helps you retrieve some money that otherwise would be gone with the wind.

We must also reckon with the possibility that the person who did, or at least was supposed to do, the work on your home has left town. One common ploy is for a home repair con artist to take a 33 percent deposit, bring a few materials over to your garage, promise to show up next week, and then disappear. You're left with maybe $50 of materials for perhaps $1,000 of your hard-earned money. If this happens to you, notify your state consumer agency, your state attorney general's office (if the two are distinct), and most of all—if you haven't already done so—the police!

Another variation on this endless theme is the roofer (or driveway paver, basement waterproofer, etc.) who offers what seems like a bargain price. It is, too. Perhaps the price was only $1,000 for a job that would normally cost $5,000. By the time you realize what a lousy job you got, this fellow has skipped town. Call the same three agencies.

One more variation is the contractor who lets you pay for his work on an installment basis (probably with a stiff interest rate). There's no hint in the price he charges that he's going to do anything but first-quality work. But in fact, the work he does is substandard. He then sells your installment contract to some finance company and leaves town. By the time the shingles start to fall off your roof, or it rains again and you find your basement still leaks, the contractor is long gone. Only the finance company is still around, demanding payment from you and claiming that it scarcely knew the gentleman from whom it bought the installment contract. For a summary of your rights in this situation, see the discussion of the holder-in-due-course doctrine in the entry for Credit Problems.

Hospitals. See Medical Treatment.

Houses. If your brand-new house has been completed, but not quite to your satisfaction, there are several places you can turn. First, of course, try to thrash things out with the builder himself. If that fails, a local builders' association may be willing to mediate the dispute. Look in the telephone book under National Association of Home Builders (NAHB) to see if it has a local affiliate in your area. Also look under Builders Association of Greater (name of the nearest large city), or just Builders Association of (name of city or state). If you still can't find a local builders' association, call your city or town hall and ask the building inspector or buildings department for help.

The Better Business Bureau may also be able to help. In many places the BBB (see II-D) offers binding arbitration as a public service, when both parties agree to it. The American Arbitration Association may also be willing to arbitrate your complaint for a small fee (far less than it would cost you to go to court). Traditionally, the AAA has shied away from getting involved in arbitrating consumer disputes, but it is beginning to move in that direction. In Harrisburg, Tucson, Cleveland, Miami, and Pittsburgh, the AAA will definitely handle consumer complaints.

If none of these resources seems to hold the solution to your dispute with a builder, you can fall back on that reliable standby your state consumer protection agency (see II-F).

If your problem is with a house you've bought from the previous owner, you have far fewer recourses. Nothing requires the previous owner to tell you about the home's flaws. Even if you asked him whether the roof leaked and he said no and then you discovered it *does,* there's still not much you can charge him with except being an evil person. Your only protections are those written into your contract or other written agreements. That's why it's so important to have the assistance of a lawyer when buying a house. If you think a written agreement involved in your purchase has been breached, check with your lawyer. If you don't have a lawyer, get one. If you don't know how to get one, see the discussion of lawyers in II-O.

Humidifiers. See Appliances and Appliance Repairs.

Inheritance. If you've inherited something, the executor of the will normally makes sure you get what's coming to you. Thus, you should be suspicious if you get a notice in the mail that someone sharing your surname is entitled to an inheritance, and it may be you. If the person sending the mail offers to check into the situation, *for a fee,* you should be doubly suspicious. In fact, you should probably drop a line to your state consumer protection agency (see II-F) and your state attorney general's office (if they're distinct), as well as the postal inspector at the nearest major post office.

If you've already paid the fee, it may be too late to get your money back. But you can try. Send your complaint to those same three agencies. By the way, thousands of people named Kelly fell for this scheme a couple of years ago.

If you have the opposite kind of inheritance problem—you really have strong reason to think you've inherited something, but it's being kept from you—your best bet is to hire a lawyer (see II-O), probably on a contingency-fee basis. That means if he succeeds in getting something for you, he'll get an agreed-upon portion as a fee.

Insurance. You had one minor accident that wasn't even your fault, and you find your auto insurance rate has been raised. Or you had two accidents and suddenly find the company won't renew your policy. Or you bought a health insurance policy, but now that you've developed a heart condition the company wants to charge you extra. Or you were turned down for a life insurance policy, and you don't understand why. Or a tree fell on your house, and the homeowner's insurance company is being slow in paying for the damage. Or you have a dented fender, and the auto insurance company won't pay you as much to fix it as your body shop says it will actually cost. Or your spouse died seven weeks ago, and you need some of the life insurance money to pay bills, but your money hasn't come through yet.

With all of these, and the many other problems that can crop up in the realm of insurance, there is one basic governmental recourse for your problems: the state insurance department.

Some state insurance departments are fast to respond, competent, and eager to help. Others are slow, insensitive, and bureaucratic. I'm not going to give my opinion of which are which, because they can change fairly quickly. A new governor usually appoints a new insurance commissioner.

But here are their addresses. Thank heaven for the good ones, and pester the heck out of the bad ones.

- *Alabama:* Department of Insurance, Administration Building, Montgomery, AL 36130
- *Alaska:* Division of Insurance, Dept. of Commerce and Economic Development, Pouch D, Juneau, AK 99811
- *Arizona:* Insurance Department, 1601 W. Jefferson St., Phoenix, AZ 85007
- *Arkansas*: Insurance Division, Department of Commerce, 400 University Tower Building, Little Rock, AR 72204
- *California:* Department of Insurance, 600 S. Commonwealth Ave., Los Angeles, CA 90005
- *Colorado:* Insurance Division, Dept. of Regulatory Affairs, 106 State Office Bldg., 201 E. Colfax Ave., Denver, CO 80203
- *Connecticut:* Insurance Department, State Office Building, 165 Capitol Ave., Hartford, CT 06115
- *Delaware:* Insurance Department, 21 The Green, Dover, DE 19901
- *District of Columbia:* Department of Insurance, 614 H St. NW, Washington, DC 20001
- *Florida:* Department of Insurance, The Capitol, Tallahassee, FL 32304
- *Georgia:* Insurance Department, 238 State Capitol, Atlanta, GA 30334
- *Hawaii:* Insurance Division, Department of Regulatory Affairs, 1010 Richards St., Honolulu, HI 96811
- *Idaho:* Department of Insurance, 700 West State St., Boise, ID 83720
- *Illinois:* Department of Insurance, 215 E. Monroe, Springfield, IL 62767
- *Indiana:* Insurance Department, 509 State Office Building, Indianapolis, IN 46204

- *Iowa:* Insurance Department, Lucas Building, Des Moines, IA 50319
- *Kansas:* Insurance Department, First Floor, State Office Building, Topeka, KS 66612
- *Kentucky:* Department of Insurance, Capitol Plaza Tower, Frankfort, KY 40601
- *Louisiana:* Insurance Department, 950 N. Fifth St., Baton Rouge, LA 70804
- *Maine:* Bureau of Insurance, Department of Business Regulation, State House, Augusta, ME 04333
- *Maryland:* Insurance Division, One S. Calvert St., Baltimore, MD 21202
- *Massachusetts:* Division of Insurance, State Office Building, 100 Cambridge St., Boston, MA 02202
- *Michigan:* Insurance Bureau, Department of Commerce, 1048 Pierpont St., Lansing, MI 48910
- *Minnesota:* Insurance Division, Department of Commerce, Metro Square Building, Saint Paul, MN 55101
- *Mississippi:* Insurance Department, 1804 Sillers Building, Jackson, MS 39205
- *Missouri:* Division of Insurance, Department of Consumer Affairs, Regulation and Licensing, 515 E. High St., Jefferson City, MO 65101
- *Montana:* Insurance Division, Office of State Auditor, 213 Mitchell Building, Helena MT 59601
- *Nebraska:* Department of Insurance, 301 Centennial Mall South, Lincoln NE 68509
- *Nevada:* Insurance Division, Department of Commerce, Room 312, Nye Building, Carson City, NV 89710
- *New Hampshire:* Insurance Department, 169 Manchester St., Concord, NH 03301
- *New Jersey:* Department of Insurance, 201 E. State St., PO Box 1510, Trenton, NJ 08625

- *New Mexico:* Insurance Department, P.E.R.A. Building, Santa Fe, NM 87503
- *New York:* Department of Insurance, 82d Floor, Two World Trade Center, New York, NY 10047
- *North Carolina:* Department of Insurance, 316 Fayetteville St., Raleigh, NC 27611
- *North Dakota:* Insurance Department, 5th Floor, State Capitol, Bismarck, ND 58505
- *Ohio:* Department of Insurance, 2100 Stella Ct., Columbus, OH 43215
- *Oregon:* Insurance Division, Dept. of Commerce, 158 Twelfth St. NE, Salem, OR 97310
- *Pennsylvania:* Insurance Department, 13th Floor, Strawberry Square, Harrisburg, PA 17120
- *Rhode Island:* Insurance Commissioner, Dept. of Business Regulation, 100 N. Main St., Providence, RI 02903
- *South Carolina:* Department of Insurance, 2711 Middleburg Dr., Columbia, SC 29204
- *South Dakota:* Division of Insurance, Dept. of Commerce and Consumer Affairs, Insurance Building, Pierre, SD 57501
- *Tennessee:* Department of Insurance, 114 State Office Bldg., Nashville, TN 37219
- *Texas:* Board of Insurance, 1100 San Jacinto Blvd., Austin, TX 78786
- *Utah:* Insurance Department, 326 S. 500 East, Salt Lake City, UT 84111
- *Vermont:* Department of Banking and Insurance, 120 State St., Montpelier, VT 05602
- *Virginia:* Bureau of Insurance, State Corporation Commission, Blanton Building, Richmond, VA 23219
- *Washington:* Insurance Commissioner, Insurance Building, Olympia, WA 98504

- *West Virginia:* Department of Insurance, Room 643, Building 3, State Capitol Complex, Charleston, WV 25305
- *Wisconsin:* Office of Commissioner of Insurance, 123 W. Washington Ave., Madison, WI 53703
- *Wyoming:* Insurance Department, 500 Randall Ave., Cheyenne, WY 82002

Job-Related Problems. (See also Discrimination, Pensions.) If you are a member of a union, most job-related difficulties (including pensions and retirement benefits) should be taken up first with your union. If you're not a union member or your union performs unsatisfactorily, the best recourse agencies for many problems are your state department of labor or the U.S. Department of Labor. Problems regarding job safety should be reported to the U.S. Occupational Safety and Health Administration (OSHA), which is listed in the phone book under the U.S. Labor Department in the government listings in the white pages. Environmental problems should be reported to your supervisors, the authorities mentioned in the entry Pollution, or both. Injuries that occur during working time should be reported immediately to your supervisor. If the company doesn't act immediately to provide you with medical care and rehabilitation for the injury, or if the injury was a serious one, report it promptly to your state workmen's compensation board.

Lakeside Lot Sites. See Real Estate.

Landlord-Tenant Problems. The tenants' rights movement made a lot of progress in the 1960s and early 1970s. Currently, the pendulum of power seems to be swinging back toward landlords, mainly because a nationwide shortage of rental housing puts landlords, as controllers of a scarce commodity, in a position of strength.

Still, if you—like most tenants—have never belonged to a tenants' group or otherwise boned up on your rights, you may be amazed to learn how many rights you have. Exactly what your rights are varies greatly, however, depending on what state, county, and city or town you live in.

Two basic protections for tenants exist in most jurisdictions. One is a ban on retaliatory eviction—that is, the eviction of a tenant in response to his or her joining a tenants' group or in response to filing a complaint with a government agency. The other is a law putting some limits on how long a landlord may legally keep a tenant's security deposit after a lease has expired. Most security deposit laws also limit the size of the deposit (usually to one and a half or two months' rent), and a few require payment of interest on security deposits.

An increasing number of states now recognize the "implied warranty of habitability." This doctrine, parallel to the "implied warranty of merchantability" for consumer products, states that a landlord, by offering his premises for rent, is making an implicit promise that they're suitable for habitation. When a state recognizes this doctrine, either through legislation or through judicial decisions, tenants are much better off. They have a basic premise from which specific tenants' rights can be derived. The implied warranty of habitability, where it exists, annuls the old common-law doctrine of "independent covenants." That doctrine held that the tenant's obligation to pay rent was completely separate from any obligation of the landlord to provide livable premises. In other words, you have to pay whether you're getting what you pay for or not. Most leases, if you read them carefully, still adhere to this outmoded philosophy. But many lease provisions will no longer hold up in court. The chief use of some parts of a lease nowadays is to terrorize uninformed tenants, to keep them from exercising their legal rights.

Once a state has recognized the implied warranty of habitability, it is only a small step to legalizing rent strikes, or rent-withholding actions, under certain circumstances. And a fair number of states have done so, including almost all of the large, highly urban states. The form rent withholding may take varies, however. In some places, it's legal to make needed repairs yourself, if the landlord has failed to do so, and to take the cost out of the rent you pay. This remedy, called repair-and-deduct, is useful, but it's almost always limited in terms of the dollar amount deductible. Often the limit is one month's rent, though in Massachusetts it's two months' rent, and there's no fixed limit in New Jersey.

The withholding of larger amounts either requires a court action on your part or invites one from your landlord. Therefore, you should undertake such rent-withholding actions only in conjunction with a lawyer, a tenants' association, or both. Tenants' associations are much to be recommended, anyway, since tenants have much more power to deal with a landlord when they band together than when they work separately. A single person making complaints or withholding rent may be at most a nuisance for a landlord. A group of a third or more of his tenants doing the same thing poses an economic threat and a force that must be dealt with.

If there's no tenants' group in your building and you want to form one, try to do so in conjunction with a citywide or statewide tenants' group in your area. If you can't find a larger group to advise you or to affiliate with, write the National Housing and Economic Development Law Project, 2150 Shattuck Ave., Berkeley, CA 94704. They may be able to help you link up with a group, and they may also be able to provide you with useful information.

Your group, if it doesn't contain a lawyer, should consult with a lawyer for up-to-date information on applicable state laws. But your strategies needn't be limited solely to the remedies the law provides. Picketing or other forms of adverse publicity can be highly effective against some landlords. Voluntary consumer groups and the media have a fairly high level of interest in landlord-tenant disputes: You may be able to get additional help there. Research about your landlord, particularly his business ventures and his other real estate holdings, could give you a splendid tactical edge. A book giving invaluable tips on how to conduct such research is *People Before Property,* published by Urban Planning Aid, Inc., 639 Massachusetts Ave., Cambridge, MA 02139.

A somewhat longer treatment of landlord-tenant problems and how to cope with them appeared in a series of three articles in *Consumer Reports* magazine (October and November 1974, and January 1975), collectively entitled "A Guide for Renters." Another useful source of information is the 1978 book *The Rights of Tenants* (one of a series of American Civil Liberties Union handbooks), by Richard E. Blumberg and James R. Grow.

Land Sales. See Real Estate.

Late Delivery. See Delivery of Merchandise.

Lawyers. A good lawyer is an essential part of a consumer's arsenal. Several of the entries in this section (Franchises, Houses, and Landlord-Tenant Problems, for example) allude to the need for legal advice. Lawyers, however, tend (as a lawyer might say) to charge fees commensurate with their training and ability. To use the vernacular, they don't come cheap.

If you need legal advice but fear you can't afford it, there are several ways of coping with the problem. If your income is at or near poverty level, you can use Legal Aid lawyers. Many of them are excellent, and most are highly dedicated. If you need only a limited amount of legal advice, your local Bar Association may be able to arrange a half hour's or an hour's consultation with a lawyer for a small fee. This may also be a good course to follow if you just want enough legal advice to find out if you have a good enough case to be worth hiring a lawyer! You can find a bar association in the phone book, under the (name of state, county, or large city) Bar Association.

In some kinds of cases, you can get a lawyer to take your case on a contingency-fee basis. That means that he or she gets paid only if you win. In that case, the fee will normally be some agreed-upon percentage of the amount the lawyer has helped to recover for you.

Also consider the use of a legal clinic. Legal clinics are law firms that attempt to deliver legal services in a higher volume and at a lower cost than is traditional in the profession. To attract the volume, they often resort to advertising—a practice that has only recently gained the grudging acceptance of bar associations. To lower the cost, they often use paraprofessionals (trained nonlawyers) to handle much routine work. Legal clinics often specialize in certain common types of legal problems, such as wills, real estate closings (for buying or selling houses), and uncontested divorces. If your legal problem is of the run-of-the-mill variety, a legal clinic may well give you service as good as you could get elsewhere at a price much lower than you'd pay elsewhere.

As a final way of getting relatively low-cost legal help, don't overlook the possibility of a plain old forthright discussion of the fees issue with a lawyer. You may find that he's willing to lower his normal fee because your case appeals to him . . . or even that he's just glad to have the business!

Lawyers, like other mortals, may have feet of clay. What's more, there are crooks in this profession as in any other. If you think you've encountered one, complain to your city, county, or state bar association. Send a copy of your complaint to your state consumer protection agency (see II-F) and also (if they're distinct) to your state attorney general's office.

Licensed Occupations. The current philosophical swing, both in the consumer movement and in the federal administration, is antilicensing. Licensing boards, it is argued, often become the captives of the industries they are supposed to regulate. Indeed, very often it is the industries themselves that have pushed for licensing. One reason is that it allows them to use the licensing boards to keep out future competition, thus driving up prices and profits. Lewis Engman, former chairman of the Federal Trade Commission, said an FTC study showed that licensing of television repairmen in Louisiana did not reduce fraud but resulted in average repair prices higher than those that existed in unregulated jurisdictions. He also mentioned, as an example of licensing boards that have turned into barriers to competition, the Florida Construction Industry Licensing Board. According to Engman, it had rejected every one of the 2,150 applicants that came before it seeking a license. On top of everything else, the argument against licensing runs, the licensing boards impose red tape on industries, thus adding to overhead costs ultimately borne by the consumer.

The logic behind these attacks is worth considering. But I do not believe the solution is necessarily to do away with as many licensing boards as possible. Where the boards are well run and include members chosen to represent *consumers,* they can provide a valuable check on unfair business practices. A board containing a good blend of consumer and industry representatives can combine close supervision and intimate knowledge of an industry with a concern for the public interest. The power to revoke licenses gives the boards a good regulatory club in the closet. And if the boards also have the power to suspend licenses temporarily and to levy fines, they have a good range of possible penalties to employ in discouraging wrongdoing. Such well-run licensing boards do exist. Some of the licensing and regulatory boards in California, for example, come close to fulfilling the model description given here. Even the study cited by Engman found that the number of incidents of fraud seemed to be lower in California, where television repairmen are regulated, than in unregulated jurisdictions. And California repair costs were no higher than those elsewhere, even though wages in California are generally above the national average.

So, licensing and regulation boards are at least a potential resource when you have a problem. The occupations that are licensed vary greatly from state to state. Some states seem to license everyone from acupuncturists to zoologists. Others license and regulate only a few professions or occupations. Some states that currently license auto repair shops are mentioned under Automobile Repairs. Some that currently license radio and television repairmen are mentioned in the entry on Stereo, Audio, and Audiovisual Equipment and Repairs. Other professions or trades often licensed are real estate agents, insurance agents, brokers, accountants, pharmacists, social workers, funeral homes, opticians, and podiatrists.

In most cases, any individual licensing boards are under the jurisdiction of a state agency for licensing and registration. Here are the names and addresses of such agencies, where they exist:

- Alaska Division of Occupational Licensing, Department of Commerce and Economic Development, Pouch D, Juneau, AK 99811
- California Department of Consumer Affairs, 1020 N St., Sacramento, CA 95814
- Colorado Department of Regulatory Agencies, Sherman St., Denver, CO 80203
- Delaware Division of Business and Occupational Registration, Department of Administrative Services, Dover, DE 19901
- Florida Department of Professional and Occupational Regulation, 2009 Apalachee Parkway, Tallahassee, FL 32301
- Georgia State Examining Board, Office of Secretary of State, 166 Pryor St. SW, Atlanta, GA 30334
- Hawaii Department of Regulatory Agencies, 1010 Richards St., Honolulu, HI 96813
- Idaho Bureau of Occupational Licensing, Department of Self-Governing Agencies, 2404 Bank Drive, Boise, ID 83705
- Illinois Department of Registration and Education, 320 W. Washington St., Springfield, IL 62786
- Kentucky Division of Occupations and Professions, Bureau of Administrative Services, Department of Finance, Twilight Trail, Building A, Frankfort, KY 40601
- Maine Central Licensing Division, Dept. of Business Regulation, Stevens School, State House, Augusta, ME 04333
- Maryland Department of Licensing and Regulation, One S. Calvert St., Baltimore, MD 21201
- Massachusetts Division of Registration, Executive Office of Consumer Affairs, 100 Cambridge St., Boston, MA 02202
- Michigan Department of Licensing and Regulation, 320 N. Washington, PO Box 30018, Lansing, MI 48909

- Missouri Division of Professional Registration, Department of Consumer Affairs, Regulation and Licensing, PO Box 1335, Jefferson City, MO 65102
- Montana Department of Professional and Occupational Licensing, 42½ N. Last Chance Gulch, Helena, MT 59601
- New Jersey Division of Consumer Affairs, Dept. of Law and Public Safety, 1100 Raymond Blvd., Newark, NJ 07102
- New York Division of Professional Licensing Services, Education Dept., Room 3021, Cultural Education Center, Albany, NY 12230
- North Carolina Secretary of State, State Capitol, Raleigh, NC 27611
- North Dakota Licensing Department, Office of Attorney General, First Floor, State Capitol, Bismarck ND 58505
- Pennsylvania Bureau of Professional and Occupational Affairs, Dept. of State, Room 618, Transportation and Safety Building, Harrisburg, PA 17120
- Rhode Island Department of Business Regulation, 100 N. Main St., Providence, RI 02903
- South Dakota Division of Professional and Occupational Licensing, Dept. of Commerce and Consumer Affairs, State Capitol, Pierre, SD 57501
- Tennessee Director of Regulatory Boards, 506 Capitol Hill Building, Nashville, TN 37219
- Utah Registration Division, Dept. of Business Regulation, 330 E. Fourth South St., Salt Lake City, UT 84111
- Vermont Division of Licensing and Regulation, Office of Secretary of State, Pavilion Office Building, Montpelier, VT 05602
- Virginia Department of Commerce, 2 S. Ninth St., Richmond, VA 23219
- Washington Department of Licensing, Highways-Licenses Building, Olympia, WA 98504

- Wisconsin Department of Regulation and Licensing, 1400 E. Washington Ave., Madison, WI 53702.

Loan Companies. See Credit Problems; Debt Collection.

Magazines. See Publications.

Mail. If a package you sent or expected to receive is lost, or if it appears, upon delivery, to have been handled by a gorilla, contact the Consumer Advocate, U.S. Postal Service, Washington, DC 20260. This is also the office to complain to for any other shortcomings of the U.S. Postal Service, such as excessive delivery time, rudeness of local post office personnel, or consistently long service lines at your local post office. Naturally, you should also complain to the local office.

If your complaint doesn't concern the Postal Service, but rather the sender, see the entry for Mail-Order Houses.

Mail-Order Houses. Mail-order complaints are extremely common: They rank fourth in my Gripe Index, for example (see Appendix I). But if you run into one, you have a number of strong recourses at your disposal.

Late delivery: A Federal Trade Commission regulation, which took effect on February 2, 1976, says that mail-order houses must deliver you the promised merchandise within the stated time, or within thirty days if no time is stated. If they fail to do this, they must furnish you with "an adequate cost-free means" of canceling the sale and getting a full refund. (A postage-paid card is an example.) If you choose to exercise this right, the house must send you your refund within seven days or credit it to your account on the next billing cycle, if you maintain a charge account with it. If you don't notify the seller that you want a refund, you're presumed to have consented to a thirty-day delay. But any further delay after that would require written consent from you.

The FTC said it issued the rule after holding hearings that produced "well over 10,000 pages of complaints regarding mail-order sales." If you encounter a violation of the rule, complain to the FTC, whose regional offices are listed in section II-H.

Other problems: Let's suppose now that your complaint concerns something other than late delivery. Perhaps the item that came wasn't what you ordered, it was damaged, or it didn't live up to the claims in the catalog or the ad. In these cases, send your first complaint to the mail-order house itself. Wait a full thirty days for a reply.

If things aren't straightened out to your satisfaction in thirty days, send a copy of your original complaint letter, along with a short covering note, to the Mail Order Action Line, Direct Mail Marketing Association, Inc., 6 East 43d St., New York, NY 10017. The association (DMMA) represents about two thousand businesses that either advertise by mail or sell by mail. Naturally, its greatest success is in mediating complaints involving its own members. But it will also try to intercede on your behalf with other mail-order firms.

Send a second copy of your complaint letter to the consumer protection agency in your own state and a third copy to the consumer protection agency in the mail-order house's state (see II-F). Send a fourth copy to the postal inspector in charge at the nearest sizable post office. With these four lines in the water, you stand an excellent chance of getting some action—and of fishing your money back up into the sunlight.

You can, incidentally, lessen the chances that you'll have to file a mail-order complaint by noting extra facts on your order form. Instead of just putting down the order number, it's a good idea to include a description of the item (weight, size, color, and other specifications). Check the company's policy on returns. If it's unclear, you may want to write to the company to find out the policy on returns before you order anything. If you do receive defective merchandise, one thing you should not do is try to send a package back COD. This would only complicate things. Send a letter instead.

Medical Treatment. Doctors, dentists, hospitals, nursing homes, and clinics have all come under fire in recent years.  Inadequate care, insensitivity to patients' needs, and ever escalating charges are among the most common complaints. But often these complaints are voiced only in the press or to third parties. Something in the atmosphere of the medical setting seems to discourage many patients from complaining directly to the institutions involved.

Some hospitals have appointed a patient advocate to hear patients' complaints and to try to see that something is done about them. If that remedy fails or isn't available, you can direct a written complaint to the chairman of the hospital's board of directors. You can also write to the American Hospital Association, 840 North Lake Shore Drive, Chicago, IL 60611, and to your county or state medical society.

The American Hospital Association, incidentally, has promulgated a patient's bill of rights. Among the rights to which that document says you are entitled are:

- The right to be informed about your condition, treatment method, and chances for recovery
- The right *not* to have that same information bandied about to other people, without your consent
- The right to a reasonable amount of personal attention from the hospital staff, delivered in a considerate manner
- The right to some continuity of care. (In other words, you shouldn't be seeing a different doctor each time you see a doctor.)
- The right to have hospital bills explained to you

With nursing homes, you should take complaints to the director, if subordinate personnel haven't solved them. In clinics, you should speak to the physician in charge. After that, you can try the county or state medical society, and the county or state board of health. Also send a written complaint to your state consumer protection agency (see II-F). That agency may be able to refer your complaint to a specialized board that regulates medical treatment facilities in your state. You might also take your complaint to your state legislature (see II-V). Some politicians have a considerable interest in health-care issues.

For complaints involving individual doctors or dentists, your county or state medical or dental society is the basic recourse agency. You may command more attention for your complaint if you send copies of it to your state health department, your state consumer protection agency, and possibly the hospital with which your doctor is affiliated. But by no means rush into a formal complaint without trying to talk things over first. Patients who suffer silently under real or imagined wrongs do a disservice to both themselves and their physicians. This advice applies to the subject of fees as well as to purely medical matters. Some doctors and dentists are willing to adjust their fees. Others are not. If it becomes a question of "Pay my fee or go elsewhere," you may be better off going elsewhere. You may find a highly qualified practitioner who charges considerably less. And there are some good-quality health facilities operated on a low-cost basis by cities, counties, and universities.

If you think you have encountered real negligence or malpractice on the part of a doctor or dentist, you can hire a lawyer to file a malpractice suit. Doctors and dentists take these suits very seriously indeed, as the recent headlines about malpractice insurance costs around the country show. Your lawyer will probably take the case on a contingent-fee basis, so you won't have to pay him anything unless you win the suit. But such suits should be undertaken only if you feel your health has actually been impaired by a doctor's actions or inactions, and only if one or more professionals in the health field have told you they think you have a valid case.

Miscellaneous. If you have a complaint that doesn't seem to fall into any of the categories in Part I of this book, it doesn't mean that you're going to have to go without help. Take a look at the complaint ladder, which appears in the Introduction to this book. For most complaints, a sensible procedure is to start with Step 1 on the complaint ladder, and work your way up gradually, until you hit on an action that successfully resolves the problem. Naturally, you can use your own common sense. With some complaints you might omit certain steps suggested in the model procedure, or use the steps in a different order than I've suggested. In any case, the complaint ladder should provide you with a reference point as you plan your own strategy for getting action on the complaint.

Missing Heirs. See Inheritance.

Mobile Homes and Mobile-Home Parks. The days when mobile homes were really mobile have largely passed. Today, mobile homes mean cheap homes. The mobile-home industry is, to a great extent, simply the low-cost end of the housing industry spectrum.

Low cost is not something to be ashamed of. It is, as a matter of fact, something to be proud of—for the seller as well as the buyer. However, some of the shortcuts that some mobile-home manufacturers have taken in order to achieve this low cost are nothing to be proud of. That's one reason why mobile homes rank near the top of consumer complaint lists in so many states.

The other reason is that most mobile-home owners don't own the land on which their home rests. Instead, they rent it from a mobile-home park landlord. This means that mobile-home owners have most of the disadvantages of being a tenant. Indeed, in many states they have fewer rights than tenants in apartment buildings. A great many states still have no laws to prevent a mobile-home park landlord from evicting tenants whenever he pleases. Having that power, park landlords can engage in a variety of other abuses: frequent rent increases, added-on fees for the use of various park facilities, arbitrary enforcement of park rules and regulations, and kickback arrangements with local suppliers (of trailer skirting or trailer tie-down services, for example), to name but a few. Those tenants brave enough to risk eviction by complaining may be told, "Leave if you don't like it here." But moving is not a prospect the average mobile-home owner can cheerfully face. Most mobile-home owners have permanent jobs near where they live; space in other parks is limited; and moving a mobile home always entails at least a slight risk of structural damage.

If you have a problem involving either your mobile home itself or your park landlord, start by complaining to your state consumer protection agency (see II-F). Some complaints will have to be bounced to another government body. But your consumer protection agency will probably be able to make connections with other agencies or bureaus faster than you could make them for yourself.

Some forty-six states have now established construction standards for new mobile homes. But only a handful of states have set standards for the warranties that come with the homes. The warranty is your best weapon when it comes to getting a home's defects fixed. A common problem, though, is that you'll be shuttled back and forth between the dealer and the manufacturer. If you find yourself in that position, try to put a stop to the shuttle by getting the dealer to agree to arbitration of the complaint by a Better Business Bureau (II-D). If that doesn't work, and the amount of money involved is below the small claims court limit in your state, file a suit in small claims court (II-N). On major problems, it may well be worth hiring a lawyer and going to a conventional court (II-O). Once they see that you mean business, your opponents may choose to settle.

The Federal Trade Commission has issued a proposed rule on mobile-home sales and services. The rule, if and when it becomes law, would require that manufacturers who delegate warranty responsibilities to dealers enter into service contracts that clearly delineate the responsibility of both the manufacturer and the dealer. When a consumer made a complaint under the warranty, the necessary repairs would have to be done within thirty days. If the defect affected the safety of a mobile home or rendered it "substantially uninhabitable," the repairs would have to be started within three business days and completed "expeditiously." And manufacturers who delegated warranty-repair responsibilities to dealers would have to monitor the dealers' performance to make sure it was adequate. You can find out whether this proposed trade regulation rule has taken effect by contacting the closest regional office of the Federal Trade Commission (II-H).

Moving. Some of the most common complaints about movers are (1) they didn't show up on time, (2) they didn't deliver on time, (3) they broke things, (4) they didn't pay fair compensation for the things they broke, (5) their actual charge was far higher than their estimate, and (6) they charged extra for things the householder didn't know were going to cost extra.

You can avoid having a lot of these complaints come up in the first place by reading a twenty-five page booklet published by the Interstate Commerce Commission called *Summary of Information for Shippers of Household Goods*. The ICC also requires a mover to furnish consumers with "performance information" on themselves. This information, amounting to a sort of report card, includes the percentage of shipments that mover picked up and delivered on time the previous year (the average, for 20 major movers as of 1978, was 86 percent); the percentage of shipments where the cost was within 10 percent of the estimate (average 49 percent, with about half the misses being overestimates and half underestimates); the percentage of shipments in which consumers claimed goods worth $50 or more were lost or damaged (average 18 percent); and the percentage of damage claims settled within thirty and sixty days (the average company settled 69 percent of claims within thirty days, 85 percent within sixty days; and 99.1 percent without a lawsuit). If you study the report cards of a few movers and get several estimates before picking a mover, you may save yourself a lot of headaches.

I'm not going to list the addresses of headquarters of moving companies here, because the companies are legally obliged to give you these in case you want to file a claim. If you run into a problem you can't resolve by complaining to the company, the place to complain is the Interstate Commerce Commission (see II-L).

Nondelivery of Merchandise. See Delivery of Merchandise.

Nursing Homes. See Medical Treatment.

Ovens. See Appliances and Appliance Repairs.

Paving. See Home Improvements and Repairs.

Pensions. If you have a problem concerning your company pension plan, your company benefits supervisor or your union is the first place to go. Beyond that, it's Uncle Sam, in the form of the U.S. Department of Labor.

Under the Employee Retirement Income Security Act (ERISA), now the nation's basic pension law, you have certain rights with regard to your pension. The pension plan must be managed prudently, so you get the benefits you're promised. You must be given a written summary of your pension plan, stating in simple language the eligibility requirements, benefits, and how to file a pension claim. You are also entitled to a financial report each year.

If you run into a pension problem that can't be handled satisfactorily through your union or employer, write to the Office of Communications and Public Service Assistance, Pension and Welfare Benefit Plans, Labor-Management Services Administration, U.S. Department of Labor, Washington DC 20210. You may also wish to telephone a local office of the U.S. Department of Labor in a large city near you.

Pharmacies. See Drugs.

Phonographs. See Televisions, Stereos, Radios, and Audiovisual Equipment and Repairs.

Pollution. In most places there are three, or even four, levels of government concerned with pollution control. If you see pollution taking place, report it to the appropriate agencies at the federal, state, and county levels—and at the city level, too, if the city in question has an antipollution agency. Local and state agencies often bear names like Department of Environmental Control or Environment Protection Agency. If you're having trouble finding the appropriate agency, your local library's reference department or the switchboard operator at your county building can probably help you. On the federal level, report pollution complaints to the U.S. Environmental Protection Agency. Its nationwide headquarters are at 401 M St. SW, Washington, DC 20460. Its ten regional offices are:

- Region I (Connecticut, Massachusetts, New Hampshire, Vermont, Rhode Island, Maine) headquarters, John F. Kennedy Building, Boston, MA 02203
- Region II (New York, New Jersey, Puerto Rico, Virgin Islands) headquarters, 26 Federal Plaza, New York, NY 10007
- Region III (Pennsylvania, Delaware, Maryland, Virginia, West Virginia, and District of Columbia) headquarters, Curtis Building, Sixth and Walnut Streets, Philadelphia, PA 19106
- Region IV (Georgia, Alabama, Florida, Kentucky, Mississippi, North Carolina, South Carolina, Tennessee) headquarters, 345 Courtland St. NE, Atlanta, GA 30308
- Region V (Illinois, Indiana, Michigan, Minnesota, Ohio, Wisconsin) headquarters, 230 S. Dearborn, Chicago, IL 60604
- Region VI (Texas, Arkansas, Louisiana, New Mexico, Oklahoma) headquarters, 1201 Elm St., Dallas, TX 75270
- Region VII (Iowa, Kansas, Missouri, Nebraska) headquarters, 324 E. 11th St., Kansas City, MO 64106
- Region VIII (Colorado, Montana, North Dakota, South Dakota, Utah, Wyoming) headquarters, 1860 Lincoln St., Denver, CO 80203
- Region IX (California, Arizona, Hawaii, Nevada, American Samoa, Guam, Trust Territories of the Pacific, Wake Island) headquarters, 215 Fremont St., San Francisco, CA 94105
- Region X (Washington, Idaho, Oregon, Alaska) headquarters, 1200 Sixth Ave., Seattle, WA 98101

Post Office. See Mail.

Precious Metals. The Federal Trade Commission has stated, "The purchase of an investment in gold is a potentially fertile area for unscrupulous promoters and fraudulent schemes, particularly in view of the inflationary state of the economy and the fascination that surrounds gold. Moreover, the price of gold is often dictated by speculative interests and is subject to significant and rapid fluctuations." Many of the same points can be made in relation to silver. In addition, no amateur can assess the purity of either metal; this has to be done by an expert, using specialized equipment. So, if you haven't already gotten involved in the purchase of precious metals, don't—at least until you've read up thoroughly on the subject.

Suppose, though, that you've already met up with one of those "unscrupulous promoters" or "fraudulent schemes." Complain in writing to the person or company that sold you the precious (or ostensibly precious) metal. Send a copy of your complaint letter to your state consumer protection agency (see II-F), and to the Federal Trade Commission's closest regional office (see II-H).

If the firm that sold you the metal is a dealer in securities, write to the Securities and Exchange Commission (see II-K). If it was a bank or savings institution, call or write the appropriate banking authority (see under Banks). If the party that sold you the metal has skipped town, notify your state attorney general's office (assuming you haven't already—this office *is* the consumer protection agency in some states) and the police.

Publications. Most of the complaints about publications, I'm embarrassed as a former magazine editor to say, are about magazine subscriptions. You send your check in, and your subscription takes months to start—or perhaps it never starts. Sometimes it starts, but issues are skipped. Since you parted with your money in the first place because you're highly interested in the subjects the magazine covers, you're now highly annoyed.

Your first complaint, of course, should go to the manager of the subscription department or, in the case of newspapers, the circulation department. If the publication is local, follow up your letter with one or more telephone calls. If not, follow up your first letter with a second, two weeks later. If after a month you've had no response, send a letter to Magazine Action Line, Publishers Clearing House, 382 Channel Drive, Port Washington, NY 11050.

If a newspaper is involved, you may find it piquant (or even helpful) to write about your subscription problem in a letter to the editor or a letter to the paper's consumer action line.

A final resort, and one that should normally prove effective, is to complain to your state consumer protection agency (II-F).

While complaints about subscriptions are the most common gripes, you may have complaints about the content of the publication. If you find an advertisement to be deceptive or in bad taste, write the publication's advertising manager, or (for large publications) department of advertising acceptability. If your complaint concerns editorial content, try to find the chief editor's name on the masthead and write him. If you think fairness or accuracy demands a correction of an item previously printed, say so at the outset of your letter. This helps to crystallize the issues involved. It also improves the chances that your "letter-to-the-editor" will be published, since an editor may propose that route as a substitute for a correction.

If you encounter an item in a book that strikes you as misleading (or distasteful), you needn't assume that the damage has already been done. Many books go through more than one printing. So check the title page to see who the publishing house is, look up that publisher's address on the copyright page or at the library, and send a letter to the publisher.

One other subject of complaints in the publications realm is book clubs. See the entry under Buying Clubs for suggestions on dealing with the problems that can arise here.

Pyramid Plans. (See also Distributorships.) Pyramid plans work like this. A gets money from B and C. B and C get money from E, F, and G. They in turn get money from H, I, J, and K. As more and more people enter the scheme, the people near the top of the pyramid are supposed to get rich.

A moment's thought will reveal that the scheme works to enrich the early participants only to the extent that it impoverishes the latecomers. That's one reason why pyramid plans are widely illegal. If you join one, you may find yourself losing money, and facing a threat of prosecution to boot. Chain letters are the best known form of pyramid plan. They largely faded from view during the 1970s. But in 1980 the same idea resurfaced in the form of "pyramid parties" held in private homes (throughout the country, but especially in California). Inflation and recession tend to make people more likely to be taken in by this sort of hocus pocus.

If you are invited to participate in a pyramid plan, or if you've been duped by one, contact your state consumer protection agency (II-F), a city or county consumer agency if there is one in your area (II-E), and, depending on your judgment of the situation, possibly the police.

In 1980 the "Circle of Gold," and the "Business Lift" were two popular pyramid plans. The names may well change. In any case, don't let an enticing name draw you into this sucker's deal.

Racial Discrimination. See Discrimination.

Radios. See Televisions, Stereos, Radios, and Audiovisual Equipment and Repairs.

Railroads. See Trains.

Ranges. See Appliances and Appliance Repairs.

Real Estate. If you bought land in another state and are sorry you did, your problem may fall within the province of the Office of Interstate Land Sales, Department of Housing and Urban Development, Washington, DC 20410. Since 1973 HUD has had regulations requiring full disclosure of key facts involved in interstate land transactions. Among the things that must be disclosed—in a property report that must be furnished to prospective buyers—are these:

- Whether there is physical access to the property by car
- Whether there are legal incumbrances on the title to the property
- The availability of utilities
- The availability of sewage lines
- The availability of fire and flood insurance
- Whether decent drinking water is available (If this is not known, the report must say so.)
- Whether a building permit would be required to build on the land
- Information on the financial standing of the developer
- Special risk factors, such as restrictions on resale of the land
- Information on any lawsuits that have been filed against the developer, and about any actions by government agencies to prosecute or discipline the developer

The law requires that developers (of fifty lots or more) tell you all this in writing at least seventy-two hours before you sign any purchase agreement. If you can demonstrate that the information furnished in the property report you received was false or inadequate, HUD may be able to help you or direct you to someone who can. It might even launch its own investigation, which could indirectly help you in getting your money back.

Besides the federal agency, you should direct a copy of any real estate complaint you have to the appropriate state agency. Finding that agency isn't always easy, though. So send your complaint first to your state consumer protection agency (see II-F). In your covering letter, ask whether there are any specialized agencies in the state, such as a real estate commission, to which your complaint should also be sent.

If the firm that sold you the land (or, in rarer cases, the building or buildings) was an out-of-state firm, file a complaint also with a consumer protection agency in that firm's state.

Don't overlook the possibility of hiring a lawyer, possibly on a contingent-fee basis, to handle your complaint in the courts (see II-O). The amount of money involved is probably sizable for you. If a lawyer can get it back, the money you spend on his fee would be worth spending.

Do not, in your anxiety to get rid of land you wish you hadn't bought, fall for the second half of a land swindler's one-two punch. Some firms specialize in offers to sell off land you don't want. They may take from you a fee or a deposit and then disappear, leaving you still stuck with the land, and out some additional money as well.

Record Clubs. See Buying Clubs.

Recreational Vehicles. See Automobile Repairs; Automobile Sales.

Referral Selling. This one can be made to sound like a golden opportunity. The seller offers you something—say, a roofing job—for a specified price. But get this: For every additional customer you dig up for the seller, you'll get a rebate. By the time you've found a few customers, you wind up paying little or nothing for the goods or services you've bought. Sounds great, right?

Wrong, as you may have discovered. The questions seem startlingly obvious, afterwards. Was that initial price a fair price? Probably not. What are your chances of scaring up additional customers, and hence qualifying for the rebate? Probably poor. If the goods or services were easy to sell, why would the seller have resorted to this gimmick in the first place?

Whether you're out of luck or have a recourse depends on what state, county, or city you live in. Referral selling is illegal in some places. Call your state consumer protection agency (II-F) and your city or county consumer protection agency, if you have one (II-E), to find out. While you're at it, do somebody else a favor and file a complaint with the Better Business Bureau (II-D).

Refrigerators. See Appliances and Appliance Repairs.

Rentals. (See also Apartment Location Services; Landlord-Tenant Problems.) Let's talk here about three distinct kinds of rental agencies: rent-a-car outfits, specialized equipment rental firms, and general merchandise rental outlets.

Let's take car rentals first. The single most common complaint with car rentals is being overcharged. Disputes over the amount owed are common—which isn't surprising, in light of the variety of payment plans offered. Unfortunately, you haven't a leg to stand on, legally speaking, if a rental clerk told you the rate would be $10 a day and 20¢ a mile, but the contract you signed says $20 a day and 30¢ a mile. Oral misrepresentation is almost impossible to prove. So, look over your contract before you sign it (even if you're eager to get out of the airport, or wherever you are).

Another common hassle is booking a car only to arrive and find that the type of car you requested isn't available—or, worse, that there are no cars available. Car rental firms, like airlines, overbook. But, unlike the case with the airlines, you have no standard remedies prescribed by statute. The best course is to be firm; demand to speak to superiors. If you're unduly delayed, I think it's appropriate to write the rental firm afterwards and ask to be compensated for your lost time.

Still other disputes concern what happens if you get into an accident with a rented car. Your contract includes insurance, but there's a deductible: The insurance won't pay the first $250 or so of collision damages. When you rent, you can cover yourself against liability for the deductible by buying, at a small extra charge, a "deductible waiver." Otherwise, you're liable for damages up to the amount of the deductible.

A last major group of disputes concerns the condition of the car. If you rent from one of the major firms, you should be able to expect a new car in good condition. If you rent from one of the lesser-known firms, you can expect an older car (and a correspondingly lower charge). But the car should still be clean and in good operating order. If it's not, you have a legitimate complaint.

One good place to complain (after the firm itself, of course) is the Federal Trade Commission (see II-H). The FTC has been following activities in the rent-a-car industry with considerable interest. (In 1975 the agency filed an antitrust suit against the three largest rent-a-car firms.) Your standard recourses—Better Business Bureau (II-D), local consumer agency (II-E), and state consumer agency (II-F) —also make sense here. So, in some cases, does a resort to small claims court (II-N). But before resorting to a small claims court on a rent-a-car complaint, you might well try a media action line (II-T). Action lines sometimes do well in cutting through the red tape at high-volume, well-established firms like the car rental outfits.

Home office addresses for four large rent-a-car companies are:

- Hertz Corp., 660 Madison Ave., New York, NY 10021
- Avis Rent-a-Car System, Inc., 1114 Ave. of the Americas, New York, NY 10036
- National Car Rental System, Inc., 5501 Green Valley Drive, Minneapolis, MN 55437
- Budget Rent-a-Car Corp. of America, 35 E. Wacker Drive, Chicago, IL 60601

When you rent from a specialized equipment firm—one that rents, say, only power tools, or only medical supplies—you're dealing with a firm that may be highly dependent on repeat business. If you are fortunate enough to control some of that business, or to be close to someone who does, you have a powerful lever. Otherwise, you must pretty much rely on the standard recourses, such as the Better Business Bureau (II-D), local consumer agency (II-E), state consumer agency (II-F), or small claims court (II-N).

Diversified rental firms are often subsidiaries of a large corporation, so a complaint to the parent company may be of use (see II-X). The recourses mentioned above may help resolve the dispute, as might a media action line (II-T). Better Business Bureau arbitration panels, where they exist (see II-D), may provide a forum for resolving disputes with a rental firm promptly.

Repairmen. See Licensed Occupations. Also see entry concerning item repaired.

Retail Stores. When you have a complaint involving a retail store, you're often dealing with a fairly large and diffuse organization. You can save yourself a lot of time and frustration by making sure you're dealing with someone in authority. Don't talk to anyone who won't give you his or her name and title. Find out who can make the decision you need. "Do you have the power to authorize a refund?" "Do you have the authority to offer me a replacement?" Such questions may speed your route to the person who can really cope with your complaint. Many times that's the store manager. If he can't or won't help you, your next step is to find out whether the store is part of a chain or owned by another corporation. If so, write to the chain headquarters or to the chief executive of the parent company. This tactic often produces a startling change of attitude.

Only after you've exhausted the internal corporate remedies should you turn to an outside agency for help. You can and should, however, use the *threat* of bringing in outside agencies to help speed your complaint through a store's machinery.

Which agency or agencies you ultimately choose is a question of tactics. Some likely possibilities include small claims courts (II-N), the Better Business Bureau (II-D), a local consumer protection agency (II-E), and a statewide consumer protection agency (II-F). Copies of your previous complaint letters to the store should be sent to the agency in question or produced in small claims court. For this reason, you should always put your complaints in writing the minute you suspect a solution isn't going to be easy to reach. This should be done even if the store in question is just across the street from you. Not only will written complaints provide a valuable record, they will also demonstrate to the store that you mean business.

Incidentally, buying with a charge card can sometimes be

an advantage if you subsequently get into a dispute about an item you bought. Under the Fair Credit Billing Act, you are allowed to withhold payment for an item that proves to be defective. That can give you some leverage in your dispute with a store, leverage you wouldn't have if you'd already paid in full for the item. For details, see the entry on Billing.

Retirement Benefits. See Job-Related Problems, and Pensions.

Rugs. See Carpeting.

Savings Institutions. See Banks.

Schools. See Vocational Schools.

Securities. In the broadest sense, a security is anything sold for its future investment value. However, the term is normally used to refer to stocks, bonds, and options to buy or sell stocks or bonds. If you feel your transaction has been handled improperly, your first complaint should go to your broker, and your second complaint should go to the president of your broker's firm. Put it in writing as well as orally. If this route fails to produce satisfaction, send copies of your complaint letter to any stock exchanges of which your broker is a member, and to the National Association of Securities Dealers, 1735 K St. NW, Washington, DC 20006.

In years past, disputes between brokers and customers (over alleged churning of accounts, inappropriate or unauthorized trades, failure to disclose material facts, and the like) tended to be resolved either by court action or the threat of it. Nowadays, there's a faster way available: arbitration. The New York Stock Exchange, the American Stock Exchange, some of the regional stock exchanges, and the

National Association of Securities Dealers all have arbitration procedures.

If your dispute involves less than $2,500, it can often be settled by arbitration within a month. In these cases, there's typically only a small fee for the service ($15 or so), the paperwork is minimal, and you don't usually need a lawyer. (In fact, you may not need to appear before the arbitrator in person; the arbitrator may simply take written statements from both sides and render a decision.) Usually, there's just one arbitrator for cases involving less than $2,500. For larger cases, a panel of several arbitrators is typically used, and the proceedings are somewhat lengthier and more complicated—but still nothing like a civil suit.

According to a 1978 article in *Fortune* magazine, arbitrators have been handing down verdicts in favor of consumers in about half the cases. Your chances, of course, depend in large part on how strong your case is.

If you don't choose to go to arbitration, your ultimate recourse is to the Securities and Exchange Commission. The SEC is a federal agency with broad responsibilities and strong powers for regulating the entire securities industry. Its headquarters are at 500 North Capitol St. NW, Washington, DC 20549. It also maintains fifteen regional and branch offices in New York, Boston, Philadelphia, Arlington, Atlanta, Miami, Chicago, Detroit, Houston, Fort Worth, Denver, Salt Lake City, Los Angeles, San Francisco, and Seattle. See II-K for addresses.

If complaining directly to the SEC doesn't have any effect—or its effect should be to get the brokerage firm disciplined but not to get you your money back—consider hiring a lawyer and going to court. In many states you may recover some or all your attorneys' fees if you win. If you believe many people may have been victimized in the same way you were, you and your lawyer may want to consider a class action suit. These are legal in some nineteen states. They're also legal, technically, in the federal courts, but there are substantial barriers to bringing them there.

Self-Improvement. See Vocational Schools.

Sex Discrimination. See Discrimination.

Short Weight, Measure, or Count. What you do with this type of complaint depends in part on how mad you are.

If you are only mildly annoyed, the simplest thing to do would be to go straight back to the store and ask for a full or partial refund, or for an exchange. The store manager would probably give it to you. And you could drop things right there.

However, you may start to reflect on a few things. While a short weight (or measure or count) may affect you only slightly, it can result in a lot of ill-gotten gains for a merchant or manufacturer. Consider the case of one major dairy, which happened to be the oldest and largest dairy cooperative in New York State and one of the largest in the nation. For five and a half years, from 1967 to 1973, the cooperative adulterated fresh whole milk by adding powdered skim milk to it. It also altered the milk content of several of its other dairy products. And this cooperative was selling milk at the rate of about 1.75 million quarts a year.

A Florida disk jockey made news when he started counting items packed by number and very often discovered the count was short. Following his lead, the staff of the *Wall Street Journal* started counting the number of items found in containers packed by number—everything from paper clips and file cards to vitamin pills. Often they found short counts in as many as 40 percent of the containers!

And the New York City Department of Consumer Affairs

estimated, as Francis Cerra reported in *The New York Times,* "that New York City consumers bought $25 million worth of nothing" in one recent year.

Reflecting on facts like these, you may get a little more riled up. If so, what should you do? Well, for a start, many cities and almost all counties have departments of weights and measures. Complain to them. You may want to hold onto the container in question or turn it over to the government agency. This may slow down your getting a refund, but it will preserve the evidence.

Especially if the goods were packaged in the store where you bought them, you may want to file a complaint with your state consumer protection agency. If they were packaged elsewhere, you may want to file a complaint with the state agency in the home state of the manufacturer or shipper. See II-F for addresses of the appropriate agencies.

Showcase Merchandise. You were told that the siding on your house (or the encyclopedia in your living room, or whatever) would be a "showcase," a model for other potential customers to see. All you had to do was let other people come and look at it from time to time. In return, you got a discount, the salesman said.

A "discount" from what? That he may not have said. If you've been rooked, you may find it hard to get your money back on this one, since any deception was probably oral, not written. But it's worth a try. Contact your Better Business Bureau (II-D), city or county consumer agency, if you have one (II-E), and your state consumer protection agency (II-F). If you're lucky, you'll get some money back. At worst, your complaint will serve to warn other potential victims.

Silver. See Precious Metals.

Social Security. Your check has been consistently late. Or it's in the wrong amount. Or the local Social Security office has turned you (or a member of your family) down for benefits to which you believe you're entitled.

These are some of the beefs that commonly crop up concerning Social Security. The preferred remedies for them are a little bit different from those for most consumer complaints.

If the local Social Security office turns a deaf ear to your complaints, write the Office of Public Inquiries, Social Security Administration, 6401 Security Boulevard, Baltimore, MD 21235.

If writing Social Security headquarters doesn't solve things, the next thing I'd suggest would be contacting your elected representatives (see II-V), especially your congressman. Elected officials are often eager to make sure that their constituents get the benefits to which they're entitled. (The eagerness may have something to do with politicians' assessment of a later payoff at the polls. If so, so be it: Anything that makes government officials more responsive to constituents' needs is a force to be grateful for.)

I'd also try a media action line (II-T). Action lines, unfortunately, often can't handle all the complaints they receive. But a complaint about Social Security may be a better bet for action than most. People at the action line service will often have a contact within the Social Security Administration with whom they do business on a regular basis. That contact may result in an efficient resolution of your complaint.

If these measures don't work, your most logical recourses would be a city or county consumer protection agency (II-E), or a state consumer protection agency (II-F).

Stereo. See Televisions, Stereos, Radios, and Audiovisual Equipment and Repairs.

Stocks. See Securities.

Stoves. See Appliances and Appliance Repairs.

Subdivisions. See Real Estate.

Swimming Pools. See Home Improvements and Repairs.

Tape Recorders. See Televisions, Stereos, Radios, and Audiovisual Equipment and Repairs.

Taxes. If you prepared your own taxes and made a mistake, the solution is simply to file an amended return. Any Internal Revenue Service office or state revenue office can give you the necessary forms.

If someone *else* prepared your tax form and made a hash of the job, that's another story. In most cases, your solution is limited to using a different tax preparer next time. But if the tax preparation firm or the accountant displayed actual negligence or deception, you should complain to your state consumer protection agency (see II-F) in an effort to get your money back, and to the Better Business Bureau (II-D) to warn others.

What if you're audited, and the auditor believes you owe more tax than you think you owe? That's not an uncommon situation. Many people give in, figuring there's no way they can get the auditor's decision changed. But, assuming you have good grounds for your position, that's a tactical error. If you protest the auditor's decision, there's every likelihood you can get his assessment reduced. What happens in most instances is that you and the IRS end up reaching a compromise.

A useful description of your rights in an audit procedure

is given in *Guide to Consumer Services,* published by Consumer Reports Books. You can appeal an audit either by negotiating with an IRS appeals officer, or by going to tax court. Tax court is independent of the IRS. It has two divisions, one for cases involving less than $5,000, the other for larger cases. The small case division of tax court resembles small claims court (II-N) in that procedures are informal, the rules of evidence aren't strictly adhered to, and you can represent yourself without a lawyer. If you petition for a hearing in tax court, the chances are that you'll wind up settling out of court at the last minute. Whether you settle out of court or in court, the chances are that you and the IRS will end up splitting the difference (often close to down the middle) between what you say you owe and what the IRS says you owe.

Telephone Company. See Utilities and Utility Bills.

Televisions, Stereos, Radios, Audiovisual Equipment and Repairs. Complaints in this realm are fairly evenly divided between the defects of new products and the practices of the people who fix the products. Television sets, radios, and stereo equipment are the most frequent focuses of complaints, probably because they're the most widely used types of electronic equipment. But other items from tape recorders to walkie-talkies, also fall into this category.

If you buy a new TV (or whatever) and it isn't working right, you'll naturally call the store for warranty service. If after one or two service calls, the set still isn't working right, demand a new set. Why should you be stuck for the next five or ten years with a lemon that's going to require frequent repairs? Demanding a new set may have two positive effects: (1) You may actually get a new set; (2) your demand may accelerate the store's attention to the necessary repairs. If these are done promptly and satisfactorily, you may decide you don't need a new set after all.

If the store's attempts to help you are unsuccessful, desultory, or unsatisfactory, I would take several steps simultaneously. Write the manufacturer. Send copies of the complaint letters you've written to the store (I assume you've been making at least some of your complaints in writing) to the Better Business Bureau (II-D), to a local consumer protection agency if there is one (see II-E to find out), and to your statewide consumer protection agency (II-F). If you bought the set on an installment plan, suspend your payments, and tell the creditor, in writing, why you're doing so.

To save you time in writing the manufacturer, here are the addresses of some of the key firms in the stereo, audio, and audiovisual field:

- Admiral Group (division of White Consolidated Industries), 1701 E. Woodfield Road, Schaumburg, IL 60172
- General Electric Co., 3135 Easton Turnpike, Fairfield, CT 06431
- Magnavox Consumer Electronics Co., 1700 Magnavox Way, Fort Wayne, IN 46804
- Motorola, Inc., 1303 E. Algonquin Road, Schaumburg, IL 60176
- North American Philips Corp., 100 E. 42nd St., New York, NY 10017
- RCA Corp., 30 Rockefeller Plaza, New York, NY 10020
- Sony Corp. of America, 9 W. 57th St., New York, NY 10019
- Zenith Radio Corp., 1000 N. Milwaukee Ave., Glenview, IL 60025

If your complaint to the manufacturer bears no fruit, it's time to pick up the threads of your complaint against the retailer. If none of the agencies mentioned seems about to help bring the situation to a head, your best bet may well be to file suit in small claims court (see II-N). The amount of money involved in most cases will be below the maximum permitted in such courts.

Let's turn our attention now to complaints that involve the servicing of older sets. Your initial complaints, of course, will go to the firm that provides the servicing. Make these complaints both orally and in writing. The latter provides a written record of the facts, which could prove valuable later; it also impresses the firm with your seriousness. If outside help should be necessary, there are several possible sources. In some states (including California, Connecticut, the District of Columbia, Florida, Indiana, Louisiana, Massachusetts, Oregon, Utah, and Vermont), television and radio repair dealers must be registered or licensed. The effectiveness of the licensing agencies in curbing fraud—or dealing with it—varies from state to state. In some states (Louisiana, for example, according to an FTC study), the chief effect of licensing seems to have been to lessen competition and raise prices. So approach these agencies gingerly. But do approach them as one possible avenue to a solution. (For the addresses of state licensing bodies, see the entry Licensed Occupations.)

Other sources of aid in disputes with repairment include the Better Business Bureau, a local consumer protection agency, your statewide consumer protection agency, or filing suit in small claims court. For details on these resources, see II-D, II-E, II-F, and II-N.

Tenant Problems. See Landlord-Tenant Problems.

Termite Inspection. See Home Improvements and Repairs.

Toys. Complaints about toys have a special dimension because small children have such towering hopes. They are not yet cynical about advertising: If a rocket ship in an ad looks like they can climb inside, they'll expect to. They are not yet resigned to poor workmanship: If a new toy breaks, they'll be bitterly disappointed. They are not yet capable of using things with discretion: If an item is fragile, it will be broken. If an item has sharp edges, children will bump up against them. If an item has small, dangling parts, very young children will swallow them.

Thus, a complaint you have about a defective toy is fairly likely to be a product safety complaint. If a safety element is involved, call the U.S. Consumer Product Safety Commission, Washington, DC 20207. The commission maintains a Safety Hot Line for complaints. The number is 800-638-8326. It won't cost you a dime, and it may save some child from being hurt. In Maryland, the number is 800-492-8363. In Alaska and Hawaii, it's 800-638-8333.

In addition to reporting any safety hazard, you'll want to get your money back. Here the remedies are similar to those for any unsatisfactory product purchased at a retail store. Complain to the retailer and the manufacturer. If that fails to produce results, get in touch with local and state consumer protection agencies (see II-E and II-F), and the Better Business Bureau (II-D). If the toy was expensive or if you strongly believe in "the principle of the thing," you can also file suit in small claims court (II-N). You may also want to complain to any TV station, radio station, newspaper, or magazine that carried advertisements for the toy.

If you think a particular toy is really bad, you may want to suggest it for the annual list of the "ten worst toys" compiled by Edward M. Swartz, a Boston lawyer and expert on toy safety. Swartz, the author of the book *Toys That Don't Care,* annually releases to the news media his list of ten undesirable toys being sold during the Christmas shopping season. His address is Edward M. Swartz, Esq., 10 Marshall St., Boston, MA 02108.

Here are addresses of some major toy manufacturers.

- Creative Playthings Division, CBS Inc., Princeton, NJ 08540
- Fisher-Price Toys, Inc., 606 Girard Ave., East Aurora, NY 14052
- Hasbro Industries, Inc., 1027 Newport Ave., Pawtucket, RI 02862
- Ideal Toy Corp., 184-10 Jamaica Ave., Hollis, NY 11423
- Kenner Products Co., 912 Sycamore, Cincinnati, OH 45202
- Knickerbocker Toy Co., Inc., 207 Pond Ave., Middlesex, NJ 08846
- Mattel, Inc., 5150 Rosecrans Ave., Hawthorne, CA 90251
- Milton Bradley Co., 1500 Main St., Springfield, MA 01115
- Questor Corp., 1801 Spielbusch Ave., Toledo, OH 43601
- Tonka Corp., 10505 Wayzata Blvd., Hopkins, MN 55343
- Wham-O Mfg. Co., 835 E. El Monte St., San Gabriel, CA 91778

Trailers. See Mobile Homes and Mobile-Home Parks.

Trains. Direct your first complaint to whomever you can find, your second to the stationmaster, your third, if necessary, to the railroad. If it's an Amtrak train, write: Amtrak, Office of Consumer Relations, PO Box 2709, Washington DC 20013.

If you have a problem with a railroad other than Amtrak, you can write to the Interstate Commerce Commission, for whatever that's worth (see II-L). The ICC should be able to help you with problems involving lost or damaged luggage. Sometimes it can help with other types of problems, too.

A long shot is to contact your state agency in charge of intrastate transportation. That agency may be hard to find: Each state assigns this thankless task to a different part of its administrative structure. Your state public utilities commission (see Utilities and Utility Bills) can probably tell you who has the hot potato.

Travel. See Airlines; Automobile Repairs; Buses; Rentals; Trains; and Travel Agents.

Travel Agents. Your complaint should go first to the agent you believe served you badly; second to the president of the travel agency (if they are not one and the same). If you meet with indifference, send a copy of your complaint letter to the American Society of Travel Agents (ASTA), 711 Fifth Ave., New York, NY 10022. If this route doesn't produce results, your state consumer protection agency (II-F) may be your best bet. Other standard remedies may also be helpful: Better Business Bureau (II-D); city or county consumer agency, if you have one (II-E); or small claims court (II-N).

Unfair Business Practices. See Bait and Switch; Business Opportunities; Contests; Discrimination; Distributorships; Franchises; Fraud; Delivery of Merchandise; Referral Selling; Showcase Merchandise; Unsolicited Merchandise; and Workmanship.

Unsolicited Merchandise. The people who peddle unsolicited merchandise must all have gotten master's degrees in guilt inducement from the psychology department of some warped university. If you keep the merchandise and don't order from their company or give to their charity, they do their best to make you feel like a crook, a thief, or at least an ingrate. Sometimes they even dun you to pay for the item they sent you completely unprovoked. But the law here is clear. If you receive unsolicited merchandise in the mail, U.S. Postal regulations say you may keep it as a gift. Period, end of controversy. If the merchandise is delivered to you some other way (dropped on your doorstep, for example), state laws in forty-five states still say it's yours to do with as you please. According to a 1976 tabulation by the federal Office of Consumer Affairs, the five states without such specific laws were Alabama, Colorado, New Mexico, North Dakota, and Utah. If you live in one of those five states, check with your state consumer protection agency (see II-F). If, after checking, you decide you want to play it safe, you can offer to return the merchandise to the sender. Make your offer in writing (keeping a copy), and make it clear that the sender, not you, should bear any shipping costs involved.

Used Cars. See Automobile Repairs; Automobile Sales.

Utilities and Utility Bills. In common usage, the term "utilities" includes the services of the heating company, the water company, the electric company, and the telephone company. One or more of these services (most often water) may be supplied by your municipality. Where that's the case, complaints go to city hall.

With telephone complaints, one resource (if the phone company can't or won't help you with your problem) is the Consumer Assistance Office, Federal Communications Commission, Washington, DC 20554. Telephone complaints should also go to the state agency that handles utility complaints in general.

With most other utility complaints, the state public utility agency is the first place to go. Voluntary consumer groups (see II-Q) often take a keen interest in utility matters, so they're another logical recourse. Action lines (II-T) are a sensible place to take utility complaints, since action line personnel often have a regular contact at each of the local utilities. Two more recourses are your local and state consumer protection agencies (II-E and II-F).

The state agencies responsible for regulating utilities are as follows:

- Alabama Public Service Commission, State Office Building, Montgomery, AL 36104
- Alaska Public Utilities Commission, Dept. of Commerce and Economic Development, 338 Denali St., Anchorage, AK 99501
- Arizona Utilities Division, Corporation Commission, 2222 W. Encanto Blvd., Phoenix, AZ 85009
- Arkansas Public Service Commission, Dept. of Commerce, 2nd Floor, Justice Building, Little Rock, AR 72201
- California Public Utilities Commission, 350 McAllister St., San Francisco, CA 94012
- Colorado Public Utilities Commission, Dept. of Regulatory Agencies, Room 500, State Services Building, 1525 Sherman St., Denver, CO 80203
- Connecticut Division of Public Utility Regulation, Department of Business Regulation, 165 Capitol Ave., Hartford, CT 06115
- Delaware Division of Public Utilities Control, Dept. of Administrative Services, 1560 S. duPont Highway, Dover, DE 19901
- District of Columbia Public Service Commission, 1625 I Street NW, Washington DC 20006
- Florida Public Service Commission, 101 E. Gaines St., Tallahassee, FL 32304
- Georgia Public Service Commission, 244 Washington St. SW, Atlanta, GA 30334
- Hawaii Public Utilities Commission, Dept. of Budget and

Finance, 1164 Bishop St., Room 911, Honolulu, HI 96813

- Idaho Public Utilities Commission, 472 W. Washington St., Boise, ID 83720
- Illinois Commerce Commission, 527 E. Capitol Ave., Springfield, IL 62706
- Indiana Public Service Commission, 901 State Office Building, Indianapolis, IN 46204
- Iowa Public Utility Division, Commerce Commission, 300 Fourth St., Des Moines, IA 50319
- Kansas Corporation Commission, State Office Building, Topeka, KS 66612
- Kentucky Energy and Utility Regulatory Commission, 730 Schenkel Lane, Frankfort, KY 40601
- Louisiana Public Service Commission, One American Plane, Room 1630, Baton Rouge, LA 70825
- Maine Public Utilities Commission, State House, Augusta, ME 04333
- Maryland Public Service Commission, 301 W. Preston St., Baltimore, MD 21201
- Massachusetts Department of Public Utilities, Executive Office of Consumer Affairs, 100 Cambridge St., Boston, MA 02202
- Michigan Public Service Commission, Dept. of Commerce, Long Commerce Park, PO Box 30221, Lansing, MI 48909
- Minnesota Department of Public Service, 160 E. Kellogg Blvd., St. Paul, MN 55101
- Mississippi Public Service Commission, 1900 Sillers Building, Jackson, MS 39205
- Missouri Public Service Commission, Dept. of Consumer Affairs, Regulation and Licensing, Jefferson State Office Building, Jefferson City, MO 65101
- Montana Public Service Commission, 1227 Eleventh Ave., Helena, MT 59601

- Nebraska Public Service Commission, 301 Centennial Mall S., Lincoln, NB 68509
- Nevada Public Service Commission, Room 304, 505 E. King St., Carson City, NV 89710
- New Hampshire Public Utilities Commission, 26 Pleasant St., Concord, NH 03301
- New Jersey Board of Public Utilities, 101 Commerce St., Newark, NJ 07102
- New Mexico Public Service Commission, Bataan Memorial Building, Santa Fe, NM 87503
- New York Public Service Commission, Dept. of Public Service, Empire State Plaza, Agency Building 3, Albany, NY 12223
- North Carolina Utilities Commission, Dobbs Building, 430 N. Salisbury St., Raleigh, NC 27611
- North Dakota Public Service Commission, 12th Floor, State Capitol, Bismarck, ND 58505
- Ohio Public Utilities Commission, 180 E. Broad St., Columbus, OH 43215
- Oklahoma Corporation Commission, 2101 Lincoln Blvd., Oklahoma City, OK 73105
- Oregon Public Utility Commission, Labor and Industries Building, Salem, OR 97310
- Pennsylvania Public Utility Commission, 104 North Office Building, Harrisburg, PA 17120
- Rhode Island Public Utility Commission, Dept. of Business Regulation, 100 Orange St., Providence, RI 02903
- South Carolina Public Service Commission, Owen Building, Drawer 11649, Columbia, SC 29211
- South Dakota Public Utilities Commission, Dept. of Commerce and Consumer Affairs, State Capitol, Pierre, SD 57501
- Tennessee Public Service Commission, C1-100 Cordell Hull Building, Nashville, TN 37219

- Texas Public Utilities Commission, 7800 Shoal Creek Blvd., Austin, TX 78757
- Utah Public Service Commission, Dept. of Business Regulation, 330 E. Fourth S., Salt Lake City, UT 84111
- Vermont Public Service Board, Dept. of Public Service, 120 State St., Montpelier, VT 05602
- Virginia Division of Public Utility, State Corporation Commission, Blanton Building, Richmond, VA 23219
- Washington Utilities and Transportation Commission, Highways-Licenses Building, Olympia, WA 98504
- West Virginia Public Service Commission, E-217 State Capitol, Charleston, WV 25305
- Wisconsin Public Service Commission, 432 Hill Farms State Office Building, Madison, WI 53702
- Wyoming Public Service Commission, Supreme Court Building, Cheyenne, WY 82002

Vacation Giveaways. See Contests.

Vacations. See Airlines; Automobile Repairs; Buses; Rentals; Trains; and Travel Agents.

Vocational Schools. You want to become a model? A truck driver? A beautician? An airline stewardess? A mechanic? Countless women and men who wanted to join these or other professions have thought to realize their hopes by going to a vocational school. Such schools are also called trade schools, training schools, self-improvement schools, or—when the course is given by mail—correspondence schools. The best such schools perform an extremely valuable service, helping people upgrade their lot in life. The worst trade meanly and greedily on people's hopes.

The first thing to realize about vocational schools is that none of them offers a quick route of entry into certain professions. No short course can make you a doctor, lawyer, or registered nurse, though a good vocational school course can prepare you to *assist* one of these people. Schools that offer to prepare you to be a long-distance truck driver are often misleading in their advertising. Those high-paying long-haul jobs are usually something you have to work your way up to, one step at a time. In fact, many truck drivers don't even start out driving trucks; they have to start out loading them. Similarly, courses that claim to prepare you to be a stewardess are usually misleading. All the major airlines train their own stewardesses.

The first thing you should do if you're thinking of attending a vocational school is to check with employers in your intended occupation to see how highly they regard that school's graduates. Employers are often quite glad to help you with such inquiries. The next thing you should do is check with your state department of education to see whether the school is accredited, and *by whom.* Certain accrediting bodies exist primarily to provide rubber-stamp accreditation for their members. They would accredit a school run by a colony of gophers if the price were right. Avoid schools that aren't accredited; check further on those that are.

You should pay special attention to what happens if you sign up for a course and discover early in the game that you don't like it. Responsible schools will provide for pro rata refunds, but others will hang on to your money for dear life. Don't accept oral promises in this area. Be guided only by the school's written contract, which you should study carefully before signing.

If you already have a complaint about a vocational school, possibly because you didn't know about certain of the problems and precautions described here, complain in writing to the director of the school. If your problem isn't cleared up in a reasonably short time, send copies of your complaint to your state department of education, the school's accrediting body (if any), and your state consumer protection agency (see II-F). One or more of these agencies may be able to help you. If not, they can probably advise you on whether you have a strong enough case to make it worth your while to hire a lawyer to sue the school.

Wages. See Job-Related Problems.

Warranties. If your broken widget is under warranty, you have a valuable tool to use in your quest for a refund, replacement, or repair. A warranty is no less than the manufacturer's written promise of what it will do if the product doesn't perform properly.

You may think you don't have any protection under the warranty because you didn't send in the little card that came with the product. Don't worry about it. In almost all cases, that card is used by the company to compile marketing information. A company can make its performance of duties under the warranty contingent on your sending in the card—but only if that condition is clearly disclosed in the warranty itself. Very few companies follow that policy.

What you *do* need, in most cases, is proof of purchase. This will establish that you bought the product, and *when* you bought it—i.e., recently enough to be covered under the warranty.

Under the Magnuson-Moss Warranty Act, which took effect in 1977, all written warranties must be labeled as "full" or "limited." A company can use the word "full" only if it agrees:

- to fix or replace the product for free, if the product fails.
- to make the repairs within a reasonable time.
- not to require you to go to a lot of trouble to get service

under the warranty. (For example, you can't be expected to lug your dishwasher back to a store or service center.)

- to apply the warranty to anyone who owns the product during the warranty period. (Some limited warranties cover the original purchaser only, which of course makes the warranty useless on gift items.)
- to give you a choice of your money back or a new product if the original product can't be fixed within a reasonable period of time.

As you can see, a full warranty gives you a lot of rights. So, if your widget is covered by a full warranty, remind the company of that fact, and make it clear that you understand your rights under the warranty. Also mention the warranty in any correspondence you have with consumer complaint-handling agencies.

In using warranties, you should be aware that a full warranty doesn't necessarily cover the whole product. A car, for example, may come with a full one-year warranty on the engine and drive train, and a limited warranty on the other parts. A television may have a full warranty only on the picture tube, and a limited warranty on the other parts. And so on.

A limited warranty is a written warranty that doesn't meet the standards for a full warranty mentioned above. If you have a limited warranty, you have to read it carefully to see just what's promised. But whatever *is* promised you certainly can hold the manufacturer to.

Don't imagine, just because you don't have a written warranty, that it's your tough luck if the product you bought falls apart. Under common law, *all* items are sold with an "implied warranty of merchantability." A basketball, when inflated, should bounce. A scissors should be able to cut paper. A stereo set shouldn't have a heart attack if you try to play a record on it. In short, things should be reasonably fit for their intended use. A seller can avoid responsibility under the implied warranty of merchantability only if he informs you *in writing* that you are taking the goods "as is" and that there is no implied warranty. Courts in virtually every jurisdiction have upheld the doctrine of the implied warranty of merchantability.

Warranties can very often be enforced with help from your local or state consumer protection agency (see II-E and II-F), a trade association (II-C), a Better Business Bureau (II-D), or small claims court (II-N).

Once you've successfully used a warranty to help you win a consumer dispute, you may want to use warranties as a shopping tool as well. If you're choosing between two fairly similar bicycles (blenders, boats, bar stools, whatever), you'd naturally prefer the one with the better warranty. In years past, there wasn't much to guide you in this respect, since the warranties were hidden inside the packages and you could read them only after buying something. Now, under the Magnuson-Moss Act, stores have to have the warranties available for your inspection. Using them might save you one unnecessary trip to this book.

Washing Machines. See Appliances and Appliance Repairs.

Water Companies. See Utilities and Utility Bills.

Water Heaters. See Appliances and Appliance Repairs.

Waterproofing. See Home Improvements and Repairs.

Working Conditions. See Job-Related Problems.

Workmanship. Complaints of shoddy workmanship rise most often in connection with home improvements and repairs. (See the entry on the subject.) It helps if you have a clause in your contract saying, "All work shall be done in a workmanlike manner." But such a clause isn't legally necessary in most cases. Under the "implied warranty of merchantability" recognized in most states, any goods or services sold must be reasonably free of defects. Withholding payment until the work is done properly is your best bet. Suing in small claims court (II-N) or larger courts (II-P) for a full or partial refund, and complaining to local and state consumer protection agencies (II-E, II-F) are some other tactics to pursue. Better Business Bureaus (II-D) and trade associations (II-C) may also be of help. As they are rarely suspected of pro-consumer bias, their opinion that a particular piece of work is shoddy should carry considerable weight.

TWO

How to Fight Back—from A to Z

When your new roof leaks, when the car you just had "fixed" starts doing it again, when your brand-new pants have a hole, you may feel like the whole world's against you. The odds, you may feel, are decisively on the side of the world. You may feel annoyed or angry, lonely and helpless.

In fact, there are ways you can help yourself—and there are people who are on your side, or will be, if you just know how to get them there. Once you realize you're not alone, once you understand the means at your disposal for fighting back, things begin to look less grim. You can translate your anger or annoyance into action. What started out as a depressing problem can become a problem you can solve—maybe even a challenge.

In this section of the book, I'll try to indicate exactly what you *can* do to help yourself, and even more important, who else is out there ready to help you if you ask. For convenience—or maybe just for the fun of it—I've organized my list of recourses into twenty-six items, one for each letter of the alphabet. Each letter represents one way of fighting back. If you have a problem, you can look at the list and select one or more methods that look promising to you. As a general rule, I suggest starting at or near A and working your way toward Z. But your common sense, and your reading of Part I of this book, will sometimes tell you to go another route. Not all the methods here are suitable for all types of problems. And there's no reason why you can't use more than one recourse at a time. However, one piece of advice I'd give is this: It rarely makes sense to involve a third party in settling a problem until you've registered your complaint directly, in writing, with the seller or manufacturer. In other words, step B, writing a complaint letter, is a step that can rarely be skipped. Always keep a photocopy of any complaint letter you write, so that you can later send a copy, if need be, to a potential ally in the dispute. For this reason, I recommend that you keep complaint letters, when possible, to one page. That can cut your photocopying costs, and it can save a lot of people time.

When you're mistreated in the marketplace, the methods you choose to fight back will reflect your own personality. If you're charming, you'll use charm. If you're intimidating, you'll use intimidation. If you're funny, you'll use humor. All of these tacks are fine, if they fit you and you feel comfortable with them. If, however, you see yourself as timid, I suggest you not follow your natural bent. Try fighting back, once or twice. You might discover that it can be fun. It might even affect the way you feel about yourself.

A • How to Make a Telephone Complaint

The telephone. Use it right and it can help you cut through all kinds of red tape. The first key to successful telephonemanship can be stated like this: Put the phone back on the hook. That's right. Don't use the phone *until* you've done a couple of other things. Gather up your sales slip and any other documents you have related to the transaction. Get something to write on and something to write with. And, most important, decide what it is you want. Most likely it will be a refund (full or partial), repairs, or a replacement. But give careful thought to which one you want. Should you demand a full or only a partial refund? Will you accept repairs on that air conditioner, or is it such a lemon that you should demand a replacement? Decide what's fair and what will meet your needs. Do *not* decide based on what would be most convenient for the store or what you think the store would be most likely to grant. Once you know what you want—and only then—you should pick up the phone and dial.

Eventually (and I grant it sometimes takes quite a while with some establishments), someone will answer. Here you face a turning point that will determine whether you cut through red tape or merely entangle yourself in it. You have to decide whom to ask for. If the store has a complaint department ("customer service" is now the standard, rather agreeable euphemism), it's reasonable to try it first. But if the complaint department can't handle your complaint, quickly insist on speaking to the person who has the authority to handle it.

Some stores have given their complaint (or customer service) departments broad powers to make customers happy. (Whenever I find such a store, I usually continue to give it my patronage; I'd guess many other people respond the same way. So you'd think more stores would do it.) But even with the good ones you sometimes have to press a little. For example, I bought a lawn sweeper recently from a major nationwide department store chain. It swept the lawn magnificently —when it was feeling all right. Unfortunately, it was prone to a disturbing ailment: Its nuts and bolts had a tendency to fly off in use like popping popcorn. After a few searches through the grass for lost parts and a trip or two to the hardware store for replacement nuts and bolts, I decided I had been unduly forbearing with the seller. So I called the store's customer service department. I explained that I was growing tired of playing nursemaid to this machine and that I would accept—in lieu of a new machine—two complete sets of replacement nuts and bolts. The young woman at customer service sympathized and said she could order the parts. They would arrive, she said, in eight weeks.

I thanked her for her concern but explained that, by the time eight weeks had elapsed, both the lawn sweeper and I would probably be in smithereens. I asked her to connect me with someone who could arrange a faster delivery. The young woman put me on hold, then returned to say she now had the number of the warehouse I could call. Fine, I said. But why didn't she call the number and let me know the outcome? She promised to do so within the next two hours. The two hours passed without a call, however.

The next morning I learned from my answering service that the store had called back while I was out. I was to call a different woman, also in the customer service department. I did so, and she told me the parts would be forthcoming in ten days, rather than eight weeks. They would be mailed directly to me at no charge.

Unfortunately, many calls to the complaint department have a less happy outcome. And many stores don't have any department specifically for handling complaints. In these cases the general rule is: Aim for the top. Insist on speaking to the manager of the department that sold you the item in question, or to the store manager, or to the president (depending on the type of business you're dealing with and the way your previous calls have been handled). The key thing is to speak with someone with the authority to make the decision you want made. Otherwise you're wasting your time.

Two things can happen now: You actually reach the person you want to speak with, or this person's assistant earnestly assures you that your problem can be handled by Mr. Smith, vice-president in charge of miscellaneous malfunctions. At this point you should start keeping records. Get the name of the assistant or secretary who's making the referral. Get Mr. Smith's exact name and title. Never speak with anyone who won't give you his or her name. Write down the names of the people you talk to, the dates and times of the conversations, and what was said or promised. Whenever you speak to a new person, ask immediately whether he or she has the authority to do whatever it is you want done. If not, ask who *does* have that authority. Don't waste your time dealing with people who really don't have the power to help you.

If you finally get the answer you want, take the time to confirm it. ("So you'll send me two complete sets without charge then? Fine. And I can expect them by August 3, is that right? Okay, very good.") Make sure your understanding includes a specific time by which the goods are to be delivered, the repairs made, the check sent out, or whatever. A promise without a date attached may be valid between lovers, but in business dealings it's of dubious value.

I suppose I should say something about what tone to take on the telephone. If pressed, I would say polite, but very firm. That works for me, and it seems to be what most other consumer-writer types recommend. But, frankly, the tone you should probably take is the one that brings *you* the best results. Some people could charm the scales off a snake—especially if the snake is of the opposite sex. Some people just naturally inspire fear and trembling. You know how people react to you. And you know what your strong points are, so take advantage of them. Sympathy, sex appeal, fear, a request for simple justice—they all have their place.

B • How to Write a Complaint Letter

Some people think that the appearance of your complaint letter is vital. They advise you to use expensive paper, or brown ink, or large type. I don't think such things count for much.

Nor do I see much value in the fill-in-the-blanks complaint letter forms available in some stationery stores. These forms may help people who lack confidence in their writing ability. But writing a complaint letter really isn't hard.

Do try to make the letter neat, not messy. Type it if you can. And do, as I said earlier, try to keep it to one page. If your dispute mushrooms into a major battle, you may be needing to make quite a few photocopies of your letter. Keeping it to one page will save you some money. Just as important, any third party to whom you might later send a copy, and who has the ability to help you, is almost by definition a busy person. Busy people appreciate brevity.

Keep a copy of your complaint letter. A carbon copy is better than nothing, but a photocopy is best, since it's hard to make additional photocopies from a carbon.

It's all right to let your strong feelings show, but don't get vitriolic or abusive. Remember, this letter may later need to be shown to third parties. Focus mainly on the facts, almost as if you were a lawyer filing a court brief. In a sense, that's what you're doing.

However, while legal briefs often bristle with complex jargon, your letter should be in simple, straightforward language. The goal is to get speedy action, not to impress someone with your erudition.

That doesn't mean you shouldn't write the letter as well as you can. This world being as it is, it's hard to deny that a letter from a person who appears well educated, forceful, and well organized will get action more quickly than a letter from a person who seems unsure of his use of the language, and therefore possibly unsure of his own rights and how to get them. But writing a complaint letter is not like entering an essay contest. You can get a fast refund with a letter that would never be printed in the *Harvard Law Review* or the *New York Review of Books.* All you have to do is convey, briefly and simply, some important facts.

Right at the outset, convey what it is you want the recipient of the letter to do for you. Do you want a full refund? A partial refund? Repairs or service? A replacement for a defective article? Shipment of late goods? Whatever it is, say it immediately and directly.

Then give the historical background of the transaction.

What did you purchase? Describe the item (or service), and give any applicable model numbers or serial numbers. State the date of the transaction and the price you paid. Say whom you dealt with, if you know. If you don't know his name, and his promises are relevant to your complaint, give a brief description. (For example, "The salesman, a tall, redheaded man who works in the major appliances division, assured me that the air conditioner would run on normal house wiring.") Say when the item was delivered or installed, if that's relevant. Say how you paid for it (installments, credit card, cash, check), if that's relevant. If it's not relevant, skip it. Keep this section as brief as possible, but attach photocopies of any sales slips, contracts, or other documents you have to the letter. (Never send the originals of these documents to anyone, not even to a state consumer protection agency. Keep them yourself.)

Then say what went wrong, and when. Here's where you'll be tempted to go on for page after page. Don't. It's pointless. Just sketch the problem in a few choice sentences. "Two weeks after I bought the television set, it suddenly became incapable of receiving any colors except green and orange. At my request, your service department sent repairmen out on three occasions, but their efforts resulted in partial and temporary improvements, at best." Or, "On July 4, I noticed the dishwasher leaked almost a quart of water. The next day, when I attempted to use it, it began to smoke. I turned it off and did not use it again until July 17, following a visit from your repairman on July 16. This time there was no leakage and no smoke, but, when the cycle was done, the dishes were still dirty." It takes only a few sentences to convey the basic problem. Let the small details slide.

You should then renew the request you made at the start of the letter, and in most cases set a deadline for action. I think it's in order to set a deadline, unless the letter is your first complaint and the matter isn't really urgent. Since a letter usually has been preceded by telephone complaints, you should briefly summarize any complaints you've made and the reaction to them.

Should you make a threat in connection with your deadline? Should you, for example, say, "Unless positive action is taken within two weeks, I intend to complain about your firm's practices to the Better Business Bureau, the Federal Trade Commission, and the state attorney general's office"? The answer is purely a matter of tactics. I think it's rude and therefore counterproductive to include such a threat in a first letter. In a second or third letter, such threats are very much in order. The choice of agencies you mention will vary, of course. Threats should never be made idly, so you should mention those agencies to which you actually intend to complain if the company doesn't give you satisfaction. The rest of this book will help you determine which are the appropriate agencies for you to use in a variety of complaint situations.

So there you have the basics of a well-written complaint letter. Its hallmarks are brevity, firmness, and precision. Its elements include:

- A request
- Details of the original transaction
- What went wrong
- A brief account of previous complaints and responses
- Mention of any warranty that's in force on the product (See Warranties in Part I of this book.)
- A deadline for action, in most cases
- A threat, in some cases

Most of the time, your first complaint letter will be going to a retailer. The retailer may in some cases be practically across the street from you. Nonetheless, if telephone complaints haven't solved the complaint within a few days, write! The retailer may well take your complaint more seriously when you've put it in writing. Also, you may need copies of the letter if you later end up involving third parties to resolve the dispute.

If you don't get satisfaction from the retailer, your next step, in many cases, is to write the manufacturer. Tell the manufacturer why you're writing to it, rather than to the retailer. If it's because you can't remember where you bought the product, or because you've moved since you bought it, say so. If it's because the product is under warranty, say so. If it's because the retailer was unable or unwilling to resolve your complaint, say that. A responsible manufacturer wants to know why it's getting complaints. If it's because the manufacturer has chosen retailers who don't stand behind their merchandise, it may want to consider changing distribution outlets.

How much can you hope for in writing the manufacturer? More than many people think. For example,* Margaret Helwig of Lewiston, New York, bought two half-gallon containers of Purex bleach and left them overnight on her carpeted kitchen floor. The next morning she discovered that one of the containers had a pinpoint-size leak and that bleach had leaked out, leaving a circle of white on her carpet. She was especially upset because the carpet had been bought on sale, and would cost $40 to $50 more to replace than it had cost initially. She called her insurance company, which told her the homeowner's policy didn't cover the damage. She went to the supermarket, which told her to write the

* This example was drawn from the Complaint Ledger of *Everybody's Money* magazine, published by the Credit Union National Association, Madison, Wisconsin.

manufacturer. So (despite the pessimistic predictions of her husband) she wrote the manufacturer. "They'll probably send you a coupon for a free bottle of bleach," her son joked.

Instead, Purex's Consumer Complaint Department sent Mrs. Helwig a "bleach damage report" to complete and asked her to supply the company with two estimates for replacing the carpet. Mrs. Helwig filled out the report and got the two estimates. She then received in the mail a check for $112.45, covering the cost of new carpeting, installation of the new carpeting, and the postage for sending in the bleach container.

Of course, you may not fare that well with your complaint to a manufacturer. But you may. In any case, all you have to do is find the manufacturer's address and take a few minutes to write. Many people seem to be at a loss when it comes to finding the manufacturer's address, but there's no need to be. Your local library probably carries several reference books with manufacturer's addresses listed. Often you can also find the name of the president or the chief complaint officer listed. Among the reference books you can use are *Poor's Register of Corporations,* the *Thomas Register of American Manufacturers,* and the financial manuals published by Moody's and Dun and Bradstreet.

For your convenience, this book also provides a small sampling of corporate addresses. Those for the big four American automakers are listed in Part I under Automobile Repairs. Those of some major appliance manufacturers are listed under Appliances and Appliance Repairs. Those of some major television, radio, and stereo manufacturers are listed under Television, Stereos, Radios, and Audiovisual Equipment and Repairs. Those for some major toy makers are listed under Toys.

Here are the addresses of some major manufacturers in a few other consumer goods industries.

Bicycles

- AMF, Inc., 777 Westchester Ave., White Plains, NY 10604
- Raleigh Industries of America, Inc., 1168 Commonwealth Ave., Boston, MA 02134
- Schwinn Bicycle Co., 1856 N. Kostner Ave., Chicago, IL 60639

Cameras and Film

- Berkey Photo, Inc., 842 Broadway, New York, NY 10003
- Eastman Kodak Co., 343 State St., Rochester, NY 14650
- Ehrenreich Photo Optical Industries, Inc. (Nikon), 623 Stewart Ave., Garden City, NY 11530
- Polaroid Corp., 549 Technology Square, Cambridge, MA 02139

Linens

- Burlington Industries, Inc., 330 W. Friendly Ave., Greensboro, NC 27410
- Cannon Mills, Inc., PO Box 7, Kanapolis, NC 28081
- Dan River, Inc., 107 Frederick St., Greenville, SC 29606
- Fieldcrest Mills, Inc., Eden, NC 27288
- Wamsutta Mills Division, Lowenstein & Sons, Inc., 1430 Broadway, New York, NY 10036
- West Point–Pepperell, Inc., PO Box 71, West Point, GA 31833

Luggage

- Airway Industries, Inc. (Boyle), Airway Park, Ellwood City, PA 16117
- American Luggage Works, Inc. (American Tourister), 91 Main St., Warren, RI 02885
- Samsonite Corp., 11200 E. 45th Ave., Denver, CO 80217

Your complaint letters, like your complaint telephone calls, will reflect your own personality. Whether your bent is toward acid humor, rational persuasion, ingratiation, or menace, some element of this can be expected to show through. And that's fine. The straightforward recitation of facts is the basis of the letter, but your adversaries should have some sense, too, that they're dealing with a human being. Once you've written one or two complaint letters that satisfy you, you may come to think of them as a minor art form, blending practicality with self-expression.

C • How to Make Trade Associations Work for You

Some people would never dream of complaining to a trade association, figuring that such groups are automatically probusiness. So they are. But probusiness doesn't always mean anticonsumer. At the very least, trade associations usually want to combat what they perceive as unfair competition by fly-by-night outfits. At best, some associations really want to improve the efficiency and morality of the marketplace. In short, they're worth a try.

In Part I of this book, I mentioned several associations that handle consumer complaints when a customer and a company can't resolve it on their own. Among these are the AUTOCAPS (for car complaints), FICAP (for furniture complaints), the National Home Improvement Council and its affiliates (for complaints about home improvements and repairs), the National Association of Home Builders (for complaints about new homes), and the Direct Mail Marketing Association (for complaints about mail-order houses). The addresses of these and some other trade associations are given in Part I under the subject heading each deals with.

While the ones listed in this book are most of the major ones with organized complaint-handling programs, many other associations may also have formal or informal programs. Look around the office of the company with whom you have a dispute to see if it displays a certificate of membership in an association. Or check the yellow pages of the telephone book under the appropriate line of business. Or ask your local chamber of commerce. Some chambers, incidentally, have their own complaint-handling procedure, which you may in some cases want to avail yourself of.

When you use a trade group, keep in mind the distinction between mediation and arbitration. A mediator acts as a middleman to help two parties solve a dispute. An arbitrator acts as a judge and decides the outcome. (Both parties consent in advance to be bound by the arbitrator's decision.) You have little to lose and much to gain by letting a trade association act as a mediator. Think thrice, though, before you agree to let a trade association act as arbitrator. You should do this only if you're confident the group's arbitrator or arbitration panel is objective, taking into account the consumer's interest as fully as the business's.

D • How to Use the Better Business Bureau

As of 1979, there were 141 Better Business Bureaus in forty-one states and the District of Columbia. The average bureau received about 540 complaints a month, and had an annual budget of about $125,000, of which about half was for complaint handling.

Some people pooh-pooh the BBB, which they figure will never come down hard on one of its own members. Those people are missing a potentially useful avenue of recourse: Some BBBs *will* get tough with their own members. And some businesses will act quickly to resolve a complaint once they know the BBB's involved.

Don't get me wrong. I know there are some businesses that shrug off the BBB's displeasure with indifference. I know that BBBs, in many cases, are too prone to take a business's word for it that a complaint's been settled. I know that BBBs have no legal enforcement powers.

The fact remains: BBBs settle a lot of complaints. Their service is free to consumers. Why not use it?

Incidentally, complaint mediation is not the only activity of most BBBs, or even necessarily what they do best. Other activities include: (1) the inquiry service, in which callers are given the BBB's opinion of a given company's reputation; (2) distribution of consumer education material; (3) behind-the-scenes policing of local advertising for accuracy—often the best-performed, though least publicized, BBB activity; and (4) arbitration of consumer disputes.

Arbitration is a relatively new service on the BBB scene. You'll recall that mediation means trying to cajole the parties into a settlement. Arbitration means acting as a judge to settle the dispute once and for all. It requires that both parties agree in advance to be bound by the result.

Almost all BBBs mediate complaints; only some BBBs will arbitrate them. The advantage to you of BBB arbitration is that it may provide a fast way to settle a dispute that could otherwise drag out for months. The potential disadvantage is that you may not be confident of the objectivity of the arbitration panel your local BBB assembles. If you think you may want to use the BBB arbitration service (assuming there is one in your area), find out as much as you can about who the arbitrators are, and sit in on an arbitration if you're permitted to. The nature of the arbitration panels varies greatly around the country, as can be seen from this description, drawn from *Changing Times* magazine a few years ago. The Long Island, New York, BBB's arbitrator pool includes attorneys, educators, housewives, and a seventeen-year-old high-school student. The volunteer pool in Asheville, North Carolina, utilizes many retirees. In Wichita, Kansas, the arbitrators are all volunteer lawyers selected by the local bar association. In Seattle, Washington, the regional office of the Federal Trade Commission helps recruit arbitrators.

Some factors are fairly constant, though. The BBB always tries first to resolve disputes through mediation. If that fails, both sides are asked to submit written statements on the dispute. Normally, the panel of arbitrators will already have read these statements when they sit to hear a case. Proceedings are informal, with no lawyers needed. Both sides get to state their case, and each can cross-examine the other. The decision normally won't be made in your presence. The panel of arbitrators (or, at times, a single arbitrator) will mail the ruling to you and your adversary, typically in a month or less. There's no cost to you for using the service.

The BBB won't arbitrate a case unless both sides state in writing that they're willing to be bound by the decision. Once both parties agree, the BBB's decision is as legally binding as any other contract and can be enforced by the courts.

The newest wrinkle in BBB arbitration is that BBBs are trying to get local businesses to agree in advance to having consumer disputes arbitrated by the BBB. More than twenty thousand companies have agreed.

You can find out the details of your local bureau's arbitration service (if any) by calling or writing the bureau. But even if a bureau has no arbitration service, and even if you think your local BBB's mediation efforts aren't worth much (they vary quite a bit in quality from place to place), I *still* urge you to use the BBB as one forum for your complaints. Your complaint will go on file and, together with others that may be received, may help to warn some other consumer away from doing business with a particular company.

Even if there's no BBB near you, you may be able to use a bureau that's statewide, or that serves the outlying areas of a major city. The addresses and phone numbers of the nation's Better Business Bureaus, as of 1979, are listed below.

Alabama

- 2026 Second Avenue, N., Suite 2303, Birmingham, AL 35203. 205/323-6127
- 102 Clinton Ave. W., Terry Hutchens Building, Suite 512, Huntsville, AL 35801. 205/533-1640
- 307 Van Antwerp Building, Mobile, AL 36602. 205/433-5494

Arizona

- 4428 North 12th Street, Phoenix, AZ 85013. 602/264-1721
- 100 E. Alameda Street, Suite 403, Tucson, AZ 85701. Inquiries: 602/622-7651; Complaints: 622-7654

Arkansas

1216 South University, Little Rock, AR 72204. 501/664-7274

California

- 705 Eighteenth Street, Bakersfield, CA 93301. 805/322-2074
- 1265 North La Cadena, Colton, CA 92324. 714/825-7280
- 413 T. W. Patterson Building, Fresno, CA 93721. 209/268-6424
- 639 S. New Hampshire Ave., 3d Floor, Los Angeles, CA 90005. 213/383-0992
- 360 22d Street, El Dorado Building, Oakland, CA 94612. 415/839-5900
- 74-273½ Highway 111, Palm Desert, CA 92260. 714/346-2014
- 1401 21st Street, Suite 305, Sacramento, CA 95814. 916/443-6843

- 20 West Gabilan Street, Suite 3, Salinas, CA 93901. 408/757-2022
- 4310 Orange Ave., San Diego, CA 92105. 714/283-3927
- 2740 Van Ness Ave., #210, San Francisco, CA 94109. 415/775-3300
- P.O. Box 8110, San Jose, CA 95155. 408/298-5880
- 20 North San Mateo Drive, PO Box 294, San Mateo, CA 94401. 415/347-1251–52–53
- PO Box 746, Santa Barbara, CA 93102. 805/963-8657
- 1111 North Center St., Stockton, CA 95202. 209/948-4880
- 17662 Irvine Boulevard, Suite 15, Tustin, CA 92680. Inquiries: 714/544-5842; Complaints: 544-6942
- 1523 Tennessee St., Vallejo, CA 94590. 707/643-5087

Colorado

- 841 Delaware St., Denver, CO 80204. 303/629-1036

Connecticut

- 144 Golden Hill St., Suite 603, Bridgeport, CT 06604. 203/368-6538 (Stamford 348-5790; Norwalk 853-2174; Danbury 792-4084)
- 250 Constitution Plaza, Hartford, CT 06103. 203/247-8700
- 195 Church St., 15th Floor, PO Box 1445, New Haven, CT 06506. 203/787-5788

Delaware

- 20 South Walnut St., PO Box 300, Milford, DE 19963. 302/856-6969
- 1901-B West Eleventh Street, PO Box 4085, Wilmington, DE 19807. 302/652-3833

District of Columbia

- 1334 G St. NW, Prudential Bldg., 6th Floor, Washington DC 20005. 202/393-8000

Florida

- 3015 Exchange Court, West Palm Beach, FL 33409. 305/686-2200

Georgia

- 212 Healey Building, 57 Forsyth St., NW, Atlanta, GA 30303. 404/688-4910
- 739 Broad Street, Suite 710, PO Box 2085, Augusta, GA 30903. 404/722-1574
- Cross Country Plaza Office Building, Suite 206, PO Box 6889, Columbus, GA 31906. 404/568-3030–31
- 906 Drayton St., PO Box 10006, Savanah, GA 31402. 912/234-5336

Hawaii

- 677 Ala Moana Boulevard, Suite 602, Honolulu, HI 96813. 808/531-8131–32–33
- PO Box 311, Kahului, HI 96732. 808/877-4000

Idaho

- Idaho Building, Suite 324, Boise, ID 83702. 208/342-4649

Illinois

- 35 East Wacker Drive, Chicago, IL 60601. Inquiries: 312/346-3868; Complaints: 346-3313
- 109 S. W. Jefferson St., Suite 305, Peoria, IL 61602. 309/673-5194

Indiana

- 118 S. Second St., PO Box 405, Elkhart, IN 46514. 219/293-5731
- 716 South Barr St., Fort Wayne, IN 46802. 219/423-4433
- 2500 West Ridge Road, Calumet Township, Gary, IN 46408. 219/980-1511

- 300 East Fall Creek Boulevard, Suite 501, Indianapolis, IN 46205. 317/923-1593
- 204 Iroquois Building, Marion, IN 46952. 317/668-8954
- 230 West Jefferson Boulevard, South Bend, IN 46601. 219/234-0183

Iowa

- 234 Insurance Exchange Building, Des Moines, IA 50309. 515/243-8137
- Benson Bldg., Suite 645, 7th & Douglas Streets, Sioux City, IA 51101. 712/252-4501

Kansas

- 501 Jefferson, Suite 24, Topeka, KS 66607. 913/232-0454
- 306 Insurance Building, Wichita, KS 67202. 316/263-3146

Kentucky

- 1523 North Limestone, Lexington, KY 40505. 606/252-4492
- 312 West Chestnut St., Louisville, KY 40202. 502/583-6546

Louisiana

- 200 Laurel St., Box 2366, Baton Rouge, LA 70801. 504/344-8551
- 804 Jefferson St., PO Box 3651, Lafayette, LA 70502. 318/234-8341
- 1413 Ryan St., Suite C, PO Box 1681, Lake Charles, LA 70602. 318/433-1633
- 141 De Siard St., 141 ONB Bldg., Suite 503, Monroe, LA 71201. 318/387-4600
- 301 Camp St., Suite 403, New Orleans, LA 70130. 504/581-6222

- 320 Milam St., Shreveport, LA 71101. 318/221-8352 (Texarkana residents call 214/792-7691)

Maryland

- 401 North Howard St., Baltimore, MD 21201. 301/685-6986
- 316 Perpetual Building, 7401 Wisconsin Ave., Bethesda, MD 20014. 301/656-7000

Massachusetts

- 150 Tremont St., Boston, MA 02111. 617/482-9151
- The Federal Bldg., Suite 1, 78 North St., Hyannis, MA 02601. 617/771-3022
- 316 Essex St., Lawrence, MA 01840. 617/687-7666
- 293 Bridge St., Suite 324, Springfield, MA 01103. 413/734-3114
- 50 Franklin St., PO Box 379, Worcester, MA 01601. 617/755-2548

Michigan

- 150 Michigan Ave., Detroit, MI 48226. 313/962-7566
- 1 Peoples Building, Grand Rapids, MI 49502. 616/774-8236

Minnesota

- 1745 University Ave., St. Paul, MN 55104. 612/646-4631

Mississippi

- 21 Barnett Building, PO Box 2090, Jackson, MS 39205. 601/948-4732

Missouri

- 906 Grand Ave., Kansas City, MO 64106. 816/421-7800
- 915 Olive St., St. Louis, MO 63101. 314/241-3100
- PO Box 4331, Glenstone Station, Springfield, MO 65804. 417/862-9231

Nebraska

- 719 North 48th St., Lincoln, NE 68504. 402/467-5261

- 417 Farnam Building, 1613 Farnam St., Omaha, NE 68102. 402/346-3033

Nevada

- 1829 E. Charleston Boulevard, Suite 103, Las Vegas, NV 89104. 702/382-7141
- 1890 Locust St., PO Box 2932, Reno, NV 89505. 702/322-0657

New Hampshire

- 72 N. Main St., Concord, NH 03301. 603/224-1991

New Jersey

- 836 Haddon Ave., PO Box 303, Collingswood, NJ 08108. 609/854-8467
- Route 130 & South River Road, Cranbury, NJ 08512. 609/655-2525; Mercer County 609/586-1464; Monmouth County 201/536-6306; Middlesex, Somerset and Hunterdon Counties 201/297-5000
- 34 Park Place, Newark, NJ 07102. 201/643-3025
- 2 Forest Ave., Paramus, NJ 07652. 201/845-4044
- 1721 Route 37 East, Toms River, NJ 08753. 201/341-8202

New Mexico

- 154 Washington St., SE, Albuquerque, NM 87108. 505/266-5611–12–13–14
- 1206 East 20th St., Suite 4, Farmington, NM 87401. 505/325-5221
- Santa Fe Division, 227 E. Palace Ave., Suite C, Santa Fe, NM 87501. 505/988-3648

New York

- 755 Main St., Buffalo, NY 14203. 716/856-7180
- 257 Park Ave. S., New York, NY 10010. Inquiries and Complaints: 212/533-6200; Other: 533-7500
- 2090 Seventh Ave. (Harlem), New York, NY 10027. 212/749-7106

- 1122 Sibley Tower, Rochester, NY 14604. 716/546-6776
- 120 E. Washington St., Syracuse, NY 13202. 315/479-6635
- 209 Elizabeth St., Utica, NY 13501. 315/724-3129
- 435 Old Country Road, Westbury, NY 11590. 516/334-7662
- 158 Westchester Ave., White Plains, NY 10601. 914/428-1230–31 (Fishkill, NY office 914/897-5500)

North Carolina

- 29½ Page Ave., Asheville, NC 28801. 704/253-2392
- Commerce Center, Suite 1300, Charlotte, NC 28202. 704/332-7152
- 3608 W. Friendly Ave., PO Box 2400, Greensboro, NC 27410. 919/852-4240–41–42
- 100 Park Drive Building, Suite 203, PO Box 12033, Research Triangle Park, NC 27709. 919/549-8221
- The First Union National Bank Building, Winston-Salem, NC 27101. 919/725-8348

Ohio

- 209 S. Main St., Suite 201, Akron, OH 44308. 216/253-4590
- 500 Cleveland Ave., N. Canton, OH 44702. 216/454-9401
- 26 E. Sixth St., Cincinnati, OH 45202. 513/421-3015
- 1720 Keith Building, Cleveland, OH 44115. 216/241-7678
- 71 E. State St., Columbus, OH 43215. 614/221-6336
- 15 E. Fourth St., Suite 209, Dayton, OH 45402. 513/222-5825
- 214 Board of Trade Building, Toledo, OH 43604. 419/241-6276
- 903 Mahoning Bank Building, PO Box 1495, 44501, Youngstown, OH 44503. 216/744-3111

Oklahoma

- 208 Leonhardt Building, Oklahoma City, OK 73102. 405/239-6081
- 4833 S. Sheridan, Suite 412, Tulsa, OK 74145. 918/664-1266

Oregon

- 623 Corbett Building, Portland, OR 97204. 503/226-3981

Pennsylvania

- 528 N. New St., Dodson Building, Bethlehem, PA 18018 215/866-8780
- 8 N. Queen St., Suite 502, Lancaster, PA 17603. 717/291-1151
- 1218 Chestnut St., Philadelphia, PA 19107. 215/574-3600
- 610 Smithfield St., Pittsburgh, PA 15222. 412/281-2260 4th Floor, Bank Tower Building, Scranton, PA 18503. 717/342-9129 (Toll Free Number 800/982-4020)

Rhode Island

- 248 Weybosset St., Providence, RI 02903. 401/272-9800

Tennessee

- 716 James Building, 735 Broad St., Chattanooga, TN. 37402. 615/266-6144
- PO Box 3608, Knoxville, TN 37917. 615/522-2139
- 100 N. Main Building, Suite 1210, Memphis, TN 38103. 901/525-8501
- 506 Nashville City Bank Building, Nashville, TN 37201. 615/254-5872

Texas

- PO Box 3275, 325 Hickory St., Abilene, TX 79604. 915/677-8071
- 518 Amarillo Building, Amarillo, TX 79101. 806/374-3735

- American Bank Tower, Suite 720, Austin, TX 78701. 512/476-6943
- PO Box 2988, Beaumont, TX 77704. 713/835-5348
- 202 Varisco Building, Bryan, TX 77801. 713/823-8148
- 403 N. Shoreline Drive, Suite 100, Corpus Christi, TX 78401. 512/888-5555
- 1511 Bryan St., Dallas, TX 75201. 214/747-8891
- 2501 N. Mesa St., Suite 301, El Paso, TX 79902. 915/533-2431
- 709 Sinclair Building, 106 West 5th St., Fort Worth, TX 76102. 817/332-7585
- 1212 Main St., Suite 533, Houston, TX 77002. 713/224-6111
- 1015 15th Street, PO Box 1178, Lubbock, TX 79401. 806/763-0459
- Air Terminal Building, PO Box 6006, Midland, TX 79701. 915/563-1800; Complaints: 563-1882
- 406 W. Market St., Suite 301, San Antonio, TX 78205. 512/225-5833
- 608 New Road, PO Box 7203, Waco, TX 76710. 817/772-7530

Utah

- 1588 S. Main, Salt Lake City, UT 84115. 801/487-4656

Virginia

- First & Merchants Bank Building, Suite 620, 300 Main St., E. PO Box 3548, Norfolk, VA 23514. 804/627-5651 (Peninsula area 851-9101)
- 4020 West Broad St., Richmond, VA 23239. 804/355-7902
- 646 A Crystal Tower, 145 W. Campbell Ave., SW, Roanoke, VA 24011. 703/342-3455

Washington

- 2332 Sixth Ave., Seattle, WA 98121. 206/622-8067–68

- 319 Columbia Building, Spokane, WA 99204. 509/747-1155
- 950 Pacific Ave., Tacoma, WA 98402. 206/383-5561
- PO Box 1584, Yakima, WA 98907. 509/248-1326

Wisconsin

- 740 N. Plankinton Ave., Milwaukee, WI 53203. 414/273-1600

E • City and County Officials Who Can Help You

If you're lucky enough to live in Montgomery County, Maryland, or Suffolk County, Long Island, you're within hailing distance of county consumer protection agencies that have outstanding reputations for defending consumer interests. Among city agencies, I have a hunch that Dallas and New York City are two of the tops.

The odds are that you don't live in one of these places. Frankly, I haven't the foggiest idea how good the Office of Consumer Protection of Middletown, Connecticut is. I've never done, or even seen, a systematic study of the effectiveness of county and city and local consumer protection offices. What I do know is that these agencies exist, and that, if you live near them, it behooves you to try them out when you have a consumer complaint they might help you with.

County and city consumer agencies are an especially logical recourse when you're dealing with a small, local business. In many cases, the agency will have the authority, the know-how, or the contacts to resolve such a complaint quickly. Generally speaking, these agencies can help you with complaints only when your adversary falls within the agency's geographical bounds. If it's an out-of-town company, you'll probably get referred to your state consumer protection agency (see II-F).

Besides using the local agencies to help you resolve local

complaints, you can also, on occasion, use them long distance. Say you live in Nebraska and have a dispute with a company in Pittsburgh. It certainly couldn't hurt, and might help, to drop a line to the Bureau of Consumer Affairs in Allegheny County, Pennsylvania.

Even if a county or city agency can't help you directly with your problem, it may be able to refer you to someone who can. So give these agencies a try. Help, like gold, is where you find it.

Below are the addresses of county and city consumer protection agencies, as published by the federal Office of Consumer Affairs in early 1980.

ALABAMA: None

ALASKA: None

ARIZONA: 3 County Offices, 2 City Offices

COUNTY OFFICES

Cochise County: Cochise County Attorney's Office, PO Drawer CA, Bisbee, AZ 85603

Pima County: Consumer Protection/Economic Crime Unit, Pima County Attorney's Office, 111 W. Congress, 9th Floor, Tuscon, AZ 85701

Yuma County: Yuma County Attorney's Office, PO Box 1048, Yuma, AZ 85364

CITY OFFICES

Phoenix: Mayor's Citizens Assistance Office, 251 W. Washington, Phoenix, AZ 85003

Tucson: Public Affairs Division, Tucson City Attorney's Office, PO Box 27210, Tucson, AZ 85726

ARKANSAS: None

CALIFORNIA: 33 County Offices (in 25 counties), 3 City Offices

COUNTY OFFICES

Alameda County: Deputy District Attorney, 24405 Amador St., Haywood, CA 94544

Contra Costa County: Assistant Attorney General, Special Operations Division, PO Box 670, 725 Court St., Martinez, CA 94553

Del Norte County: Division of Consumer Affairs, 2650 Washington Blvd., Crescent City, CA 95531

Fresno County: Department of Weights, Measures and Consumer Protection, 4535 E. Hamilton Ave., Fresno, CA 93702. Also, Consumer Fraud Division, District Attorney's Office, Courthouse, 1100 Van Ness Ave., Fresno, CA 93721

Kern County: Deputy District Attorney, Consumer Unit, 1415 Truxton Ave., Bakersfield, CA 93301

Los Angeles County: Consumer and Environment Protection Division, District Attorney's Office, 540 Hall of Records, 320 W. Temple, Los Angeles, CA 90012. Also, Department of Consumer Affairs, 500 W. Temple St., Room B-96, Los Angeles, CA 90012

Madera County: Consumer Protection Unit, Madera County Weights and Measures, 902 N. Gateway Drive, Madera, CA 93637

Mendocino County: Deputy District Attorney, Consumer Unit, PO Box 1000, Ukiah, CA 95482

Napa County: Deputy District Attorney, Consumer Affairs Division, 1125 3d St., Napa, CA 94558

Orange County: Deputy District Attorney, Major Fraud and Economic Crime Unit, District Attorney's Office, PO Box 808, 700 Civic Center Drive W., Santa Ana, CA 92702. Also, Office of Consumer Affairs, 511 N. Sycamore St., Santa Ana, CA 92701

Riverside County: Deputy District Attorney, Economic Crime Division, District Attorney's Office, PO Box 1148, Riverside, CA 92502

Sacramento County: Supervising Deputy District Attorney, District Attorney's Fraud Division, PO Box 749, Sacramento, CA 95804. Also, Director, Consumer Protection Bureau, 827 7th St., Room 43, Sacramento, CA 95814

San Diego County: Director, Consumer Fraud Division, District Attorney's Office, PO Box X-1011, San Diego, CA 92112

San Francisco County: Assistant District Attorney, Consumer Fraud, Economic Crime Unit, District Attorney's Office, 880 Bryant St., Room 320, San Francisco, CA 94103

San Joaquin County: Deputy District Attorney, PO Box 50, Stockton, CA 95201

San Luis Obispo County: District Attorney, Consumer Unit, District Attorney's Office, 302 Courthouse Annex, San Luis Obispo, CA 93408

San Mateo County: Deputy District Attorney, Hall of Justice and Records, Redwood City, CA 94063

Santa Barbara County: Deputy District Attorney, Consumer Business Law Section, 118 E. Figueroa, Santa Barbara, CA 93101

Santa Clara County: Department of Consumer Affairs, 1555 Berger Drive, San Jose, CA 95112. Also, Consumer Fraud Unit, District Attorney's Office, 70 W. Hedding St., West Wing, San Jose, CA 95110

Santa Cruz County: Office of District Attorney, Division of Consumer Affairs, County Building, 701 Ocean St., Room 240, Santa Cruz, CA 95060. Also, Consumer Protection Unit, District Attorney's Office, PO Box 1159, 701 Ocean St., Santa Cruz, CA 95061

Solano County: Deputy District Attorney, Consumer Fraud Union, 600 Union Ave., Fairfield, CA 94533

Stanislaus County: Office of Consumer Affairs, 921 County Center Number 3 Court, Room 60, Modesto, CA 95355. Also, Deputy District Attorney, Consumer Fraud Unit, PO Box 442, Modesto, CA 95353

Sutter County: Office of Consumer Affairs, Dept. of Weights and Measures, 142 Garden Highway, Yuba City, CA 95991

Ventura County: Deputy District Attorney, Consumer Fraud Section, 800 S. Victoria Ave., Ventura, CA 93009

Yolo County: District Attorney, Consumer Fraud Division, PO Box 412, Woodland, CA 95695

CITY OFFICES

Los Angeles: Director, Consumer Protection Section, Assistant City Attorney, 1700 City Hall East, 200 N. Main St., Los Angeles, CA 90012

San Diego: Consumer Protection Unit, City Attorney's Office, 1200 Third Ave., San Diego, CA 92101

Santa Monica: Consumer Affairs Specialist, City Attorney's Office, Consumer Division, 1685 Main St., Santa Monica, CA 90401

COLORADO: 7 County Offices (for 13 counties), no City Offices

Archuleta, LaPlata, and San Juan Counties: District Attorney, PO Box 1062, Durango, CO 81301

Adams, Arapahoe, Denver, and Jefferson Counties: Executive Director, Metro District Attorney's Consumer Office, 625 South Broadway, Denver, CO 80209

Boulder County: District Attorney's Consumer Office, PO Box 471, Boulder, CO 80903

El Paso and Teller Counties: District Attorney's Consumer Office, 27 E. Vermijo, Suite 413, County Office Building, Colorado Springs, CO 80903

Larimer County: District Attorney's Consumer Office,

Rocky Mountain Bank Building, PO Box 1969, Fort Collins, CO 80522

Pueblo County: District Attorney's Consumer Office, Courthouse, 10th and Main Sts., Pueblo, CO 81003

Weld County: District Attorney's Consumer Office, PO Box 1167, Greeley, CO 80632

CONNECTICUT: No County Offices, One City Office

Middletown: Office of Consumer Protection, City Hall, Middletown, CN 06115

DELAWARE: None

DISTRICT OF COLUMBIA: DC Office of Consumer Protection, 1424 K Street NW, Washington DC 20005

FLORIDA: 13 County Offices (for 11 counties), 2 City Offices

COUNTY OFFICES

Brevard County: Consumer Fraud Division, State Attorney's Office, County Courthouse, Titusville, FL 32780

Broward County: Consumer Affairs Division, 236 SE 1st Ave., 6th Floor, Fort Lauderdale, FL 33301

Dade County: Consumer Protection Division, Metro Dade County, 140 W. Flagler St., 16th Floor, Miami, FL 33130. There are three other offices: South Dade Government Center, 10710 SW 211th St., Miami, FL 33189; Assistant State Attorney, Consumer Fraud Division, Office of State Attorney, 1351 NW 12th St., Miami, FL 33125; and Consumer Advocate, Metropolitan Dade County, 140 W. Flagler St., 16th Floor, Miami, FL 33130

Manatee, Sarasota, and Desoto Counties: Office of State Attorney, 2070 Main St., Sarasota, FL 33577

Duval County: Consumer Affairs Officer, Division of Consumer Affairs, Dept. of Human Resources, 614 City Hall, Jacksonville, FL 32202

Hillsborough County: Hillsborough County Dept. Consumer Affairs, 3725 Grace St., Tampa, FL 33607

Palm Beach County: Department of Consumer Affairs, 301 N. Olive Ave., W. Palm Beach, FL 33401. Also, Chief of Economic Crime Unit, Office of State Attorney, PO Drawer 2905, W. Palm Beach, FL 33402

Pinellas County: Office of Consumer Affairs, Office of State Attorney, 801 West Bay Drive, Suite 610, Largo, FL 33540

Seminole County: Consumer Fraud Division, Office of State Attorney, 149 Seminole County Courthouse, Stanford, FL 32771

CITY OFFICES

Lauderhill: Consumer Affairs Committee, 1080 NW 47th Ave., Lauderhill, FL 33313

Tamarac: Board of Consumer Affairs, City of Tamarac, 5811 NW 88th Ave., Tamarac, FL 33321

GEORGIA: No County Offices, One City Office

Atlanta: Office of Consumer Affairs, City Hall, Memorial Drive Annex, 121 Memorial Drive SW, Atlanta, GA 30303

HAWAII: None

IDAHO: None

ILLINOIS: 2 County Offices, 1 City Office

COUNTY OFFICES

Cook County: Consumer Complaint Division, Office of State's Attorney, 303 Daley Center, Chicago, IL 60602

Madison County: Office of State's Attorney, 103 Purcell St., 3d Floor, Edwardsville, IL 62025

CITY OFFICE

Chicago: Department of Consumer Services, 121 N. LaSalle St., Room 808, Chicago, IL 60602

INDIANA: 3 County Offices, 1 City Office

COUNTY OFFICES

Lake County: Prosecuting Attorney, 2293 N. Main St., Crown Point, IN 46307

Marion County: Prosecuting Attorney, 560 City-County Building, Indianapolis, IN 46204

Vanderburg County: Civic Center Complex—Courts Building, Evansville, IN 47708

CITY OFFICE

Gary: Office of Consumer Affairs, Annex East, 1100 Massachusetts, Gary, IN 46407

IOWA: None

KANSAS: 3 County Offices, 2 City Offices

COUNTY OFFICES

Johnson County: Assistant District Attorney and Head, Consumer Fraud Division, Johnson County Courthouse, Box 728, Olathe, KS 66061

Sedgwick County: Consumer Fraud and Economic Crime Division, District Attorney's Office, Sedgwick County Courthouse, Wichita, KS 67203

Shawnee County: Assistant District Attorney for Consumer Affairs, 212 Shawnee County Courthouse, Topeka, KS 66603

CITY OFFICES

Kansas City: Department of Consumer Affairs, 701 N. 7th St., Room 969, Kansas City, KS 66101

Topeka: Consumer Protection Division, City Attorney's Office, 215 E. 7th St., Topeka, KS 66603

KENTUCKY: 1 County Office, 2 City Offices

COUNTY OFFICE

Jefferson County: Consumer Protection Department, 208 S. Fifth St., Room 401, Louisville, KY 40202

CITY OFFICES

Louisville: Department of Consumer Affairs, 701 W. Jefferson St., Louisville, KY 40202

Owensboro: Consumer Affairs Commission, 101 E. 4th St., Owensboro, KY 42301

LOUISIANA: 2 County Offices, 1 City Office

COUNTY OFFICES

East Baton Rouge Parish: Consumer Protection Center, 304 Old Courthouse Building, PO Box 1471, 215 St. Louis Ave., Baton Rouge, LA 70821

Jefferson Parish: Consumer Protection and Commercial Fraud Division, District Attorney's Office, New Courthouse Annex, 5th Floor, Gretna, LA 70053

CITY OFFICE

New Orleans: Mayor's Office of Consumer Affairs, City Hall, 1300 Perdido, New Orleans, LA 70112

MAINE: None

MARYLAND: 5 County Offices, No City Offices

Anne Arundel County: Board of Consumer Affairs, Arundel Center, Annapolis, MD 21401

Baltimore County: Assistant State Attorney, Major Fraud Unit, 309 Court House, Baltimore, MD 21202 (major cases only)

Howard County: Howard County Office of Consumer Affairs, Carroll Building, 3450 Courthouse Drive, Ellicott City, MD 21043

Montgomery County: Office of Consumer Affairs, 611 Rockville Pike, Rockville, MD 20852

Prince George's County: Consumer Protection Commission, 1142 County Administration Building, Upper Marlboro, MD 20870

MASSACHUSETTS: 3 County Offices, 3 City Offices

COUNTY OFFICES

Franklin County: Consumer Protection Agency, District Attorney's Office, Courthouse, Greenfield, MA 01301

Hampden County: Consumer Action Center, 721 State St., Springfield, MA 01109

Hampshire County: Consumer Protection Agency, District Attorney's Office, Courthouse, Northampton, MA 01060

CITY OFFICES

Boston: Boston Consumers' Council, 182 Tremont St., 4th Floor, Boston, MA 02111

Fitchburg: Legal Services, Inc., 455 Main St., Fitchburg, MA 01420

Lowell: Community Team Work, Consumer Division, 10 Bridge St., Lowell, MA 01852

MICHIGAN: 5 County Offices, 2 City Offices

COUNTY OFFICES

Bay County: Prosecuting Attorney, Consumer Protection Unit, Bay County Building, Bay City, MI 48706

Genesee County: Assistant Prosecuting Attorney and Chief, Consumer Fraud Unit, 100 Courthouse, Flint, MI 48502

Macomb County: Consumer Fraud Unit, Office of Prosecuting Attorney, Macomb Court Building, 6th Floor, Mt. Clemens, MI 48043

Washtenaw County: Consumer Action Center, Consumer Protection Division, Office of Prosecuting Attorney, 120 Catherine St., PO Box 8645, Ann Arbor, MI 48107

Wayne County: Consumer Protection Agency, Office of Prosecuting Attorney, Murphy Hall of Justice, 1441 St. Antoine St., Detroit, MI 48226

CITY OFFICES

Dearborn: Consumer Affairs Commission, 13615 Michigan Ave., Dearborn, MI 48126

Detroit: City Consumer Affairs Department, 1600 Cadillac Tower, Detroit, MI 48226

MINNESOTA: 1 County Office, 1 City Office

COUNTY OFFICE

Hennepin County: Assistant County Attorney, Citizen Protection and Economic Crime Division, C 2000 County Government Center, Minneapolis, MN 55487

CITY OFFICE

Minneapolis: Consumer Affairs Division, Department of Licenses and Consumer Services, 101 A City Hall, Minneapolis, MN 55415

MISSISSIPPI: None

MISSOURI: No County Offices, One City Office

Kansas City: Action Center—Consumer Affairs Department, 414 E. 12th St., Kansas City, MO 64106

MONTANA: One County Office, No City Offices

Missoula County: Missoula County Attorney, County Courthouse, Missoula, MT 59801

NEBRASKA: One County Office, No City Offices

Douglas County: Consumer Fraud Division, County Attorney's Office, 909 Omaha-Douglas Civic Center, Omaha, NB 68183

NEVADA: One County Office, No City Offices

Washoe County: Consumer Protection Division, District Attorney's Office, PO Box 11130, Reno, NV 89520

NEW HAMPSHIRE: None

NEW JERSEY: 15 County Offices, 2 City Offices

COUNTY OFFICES

Atlantic County: Office of Consumer Affairs, 1601 Atlantic Ave., Atlantic City, NJ 08401

Bergen County: Office of Consumer Affairs, 355 Main St., Hackensack, NJ 07601

Burlington County: Office of Consumer Affairs, 54 Grant St., Mount Holly, NJ 08060

Camden County: Office of Consumer Affairs, 600 Market St., Camden County Admin. Building, Camden, NJ 08101

Cumberland County: Department of Weights and Measures and Consumer Protection, 788 E. Commerce St., Bridgeton, NJ 08302

Hudson County: Office of Consumer Affairs, County Courthouse, 595 Newark Ave., Jersey City, NJ 07306

Hunterdon County: Office of Consumer Affairs, Skyview, R.D., Lebanon, NJ 08833

Mercer County: Division of Consumer Affairs, County Administration Building, 640 S. Broad St., Trenton, NJ 08607

Middlesex County: Office of Consumer Affairs, 841 Georges Road, North Brunswick, NJ 08902

Morris County: Office of Consumer Affairs, Morris County Administration Building, Ann Street, Morristown, NJ 07960

Monmouth County: Office of Consumer Affairs, Hall of Records, Main St., Freehold, NJ 07728

Ocean County: Department of Consumer Affairs, C.N. 2191, Toms River, NJ 08753

Passaic County: Consumer Affairs Division, Administration Building, 309 Pennsylvania Ave., Paterson, NJ 07503

Somerset County: Department of Consumer Affairs, County Administration Building, Somerville, NJ 08876

Union County: Division of Consumer Affairs, 300 N. Avenue East, PO Box 186, Westfield, NJ 07091

CITY OFFICES

Fort Lee: Consumer Protection Board, 309 Main St., Fort Lee, NJ 07024

Paterson: Department of Human Resources, Consumer Affairs, 1 W. Broadway, Paterson, NJ 07505

NEW MEXICO: 2 County Offices, No City Offices

Bernalillo County: Consumer Affairs Division, District Attorney's Office, Public Services Division, 415 Tijeras, Albuquerque, NM 87102

Valencia County: Assistant District Attorney for Consumer Protection, PO Box 718, Los Lunas, NM 87031

NEW YORK: 18 County Offices (in 14 counties), 13 City Offices

COUNTY OFFICES

Erie County: Consumer Fraud Bureau, District Attorney's Office, 25 Delaware Ave., Buffalo, NY 14202. Also, Consumer Protection Committee, 95 Franklin St., Buffalo, NY 14202

Kings County: Assistant District Attorney General in Charge, Consumer Frauds and Economic Crimes Bureau, Municipal Building, 210 Joralemon St., Brooklyn, NY 11201 (complaints of criminal nature only)

Nassau County: Office of Consumer Affairs, 160 Old Country Road, Minneola, NY 11501. Also, Assistant District Attorney, Commercial Frauds Bureau, 1425 Old Country Road, Plainview, NY 11803

Oneida County: Consumer Advocate, County Office Building, 800 Park Ave., Utica, NY 13501

Onondaga County: Office of Consumer Affairs, County Civic Center, 421 Montgomery St., Syracuse, NY 13202

Orange County: Department of Weights and Measures and Consumer Affairs, 99 Main St., Orange County Courthouse Annex, Goshen, NY 10924. Also, District Attorney's Office of Consumer Affairs, County Government Center, Goshen, NY 10924

Putnam County: Department of Consumer Affairs, 206 County Office Building, Carmel, NY 10512

Rensselaer County: Director, Citizens Affairs, 1600 7th Ave., Troy, NY 12180

Rockland County: Office of Consumer Protection, County Office Building, 18 New Hempstead Road, New City, NY 10956

Steuben County: Department of Weights and Measures and Consumer Affairs, 19 E. Morris St., Bath, NY 14810

Suffolk County: Department of Consumer Affairs, Suffolk County Center, Veterans Memorial Highway, Hauppauge, NY 11787

Ulster County: Consumer Fraud Bureau, 285 Wall St., Kingston, NY 12401

Warren County: Director of Weights and Measures and Consumer Protection, Municipal Center, Lake George, NY 12845

Westchester County: Frauds Bureau, District Attorney's Office, 111 Grove St., County Courthouse, White Plains, NY 10601. Also, Office of Consumer Affairs, County Office Building, White Plains, NY 10601

CITY OFFICES

Babylon: Babylon Consumer Protection Board, 200 E. Sunrise Highway, Lindenhurst, NY 11757

Colonie: Colonie Consumer Protection Agency, Memorial Town Hall, Newtonville, NY 12128

Croton-on-Hudson: Consumer Affairs Bureau, Town of

Cortlandt, Municipal Building, Croton-on-Hudson, NY 10520

Greenburgh: Greenburgh Consumer Board, Town of Greenburgh, PO Box 205, Elmsford, NY 10523

Huntington: Consumer Protection Board, 423 Park Ave., Huntington, NY 11743

Mount Vernon: Office of Consumer Affairs, City Hall, Mount Vernon, NY 10550

New York City: Department of Consumer Affairs, 80 Lafayette St., New York, NY 10013. There are five neighborhood offices in Brooklyn, Queens, the Bronx, East Harlem, and Staten Island. Addresses of these are 185 Montague St., Brooklyn, NY 11201; 120-55 Queens Blvd., Room 203, Kew Gardens, NY 11424; 1932 Arthur Ave., Bronx, NY 10457; 227 E. 116th St., New York, NY 10029; and Staten Island Bureau Hall, Staten Island, NY 10301

Orangeburg: Consumer Proection Board, Orangeburg Town Hall, 26 Orangeburg Road, Orangeburg, NY 10962

Oswego: Office of Consumer Affairs, 104 City Hall, Naval Militia Building, Lake St., Oswego, NY 13126

Ramapo: Consumer Protection Board, Ramapo Town Hall, Route 59, Suffern, NY 10901

Schenectady: Bureau of Consumer Protection, 22 City Hall, Jay Street, Schenectady, NY 12305

Syracuse: Consumer Affairs Office, 422 City Hall, 223 E. Washington St., Syracuse, NY 13202

Yonkers: Office of Consumer Protection, 201 Palisade Ave., Yonkers, NY 10703

NORTH CAROLINA: None

NORTH DAKOTA: One County Office, No City Offices

Quad Counties: Quad Counties Community Action Agency, 27½ S. Third, Grand Forks, ND 58201

OHIO: 8 County Offices, 8 City Offices

COUNTY OFFICES

Franklin County: Economic Crime Division, Office of Prosecuting Attorney, Hall of Justice, 369 S. High St., Columbus, OH 43215

Greene County: Consumer Protection and Education Office, 194 E. Church St., Xenia, OH 45385

Lake County: Consumer Protection Division, Office of Prosecuting Attorney, Lake County Courthouse, Painesville, OH 44077

Mahoning County: Consumer Fraud Division, County Prosecutor's Office, County Courthouse, 120 Market St., Youngstown, OH 44503

Medina County: County Prosecutor's Office, 215 Washington St., Medina, OH 44256

Montgomery County: Assistant Prosecuting Attorney, Fraud Section, County Courts Building, 41 N. Perry, Dayton, OH 45422

Portage County: Consumer Protection Division, County Prosecutor's Office, 247 S. Chestnut St., Ravenna, OH 44266

Summit County: Bureau of Investigations, 53 E. Center St., Akron, OH 44308

CITY OFFICES

Akron: Division of Weights and Measures and Consumer Protection, 1420 Triplett Blvd., Akron, OH 44306

Canton: City Sealer and Commissioner of Consumer Protection, 919 Walnut Ave. NE, Canton, OH 44704

Cincinnati: Consumer Protection Division, City Solicitor's Office, 236 City Hall, Cincinnati, OH 45202

Cleveland: Office of Consumer Affairs, 119 City Hall, 601 Lakeside Ave., Cleveland, OH 44114

Columbus: Director of Community Services, 50 West Gay St., 3d floor, Columbus, OH 43215

Dayton: Consumer Advocate, Division of Consumer Services, 7 E. 4th St., Room 824, Dayton, OH 45402

Toledo: Consumer Protection Agency, 151 N. Michigan Ave., Toledo, OH 43624

Youngstown: Division of Consumer Affairs, Mill Creek Community Center, 496 Glenwood Ave., Youngstown, OH 44502

OKLAHOMA: None

OREGON: None

PENNSYLVANIA: 12 County Offices, 2 City Offices (for 1 City)

COUNTY OFFICES

Allegheny County: Bureau of Consumer Affairs, 320 Jones Law Annex, 311 Ross St., Pittsburgh, PA 15219

Armstrong County: Armstrong Consumer Protection, Community Action Agency, 125 Queen St., Kittanning, PA 16201

Berks County: Consumer Action of Berks County Inc., City Hall, 8th and Washington, Reading, PA 19601

Bucks County: Bucks County Department of Consumer Protection, Administration Annex, Broad and Union Streets, Doylestown, PA 18901

Carbon County: Carbon County Action Committee, Consumer Referral Service, 61 Broadway, Jim Thorpe, PA 18229

Cumberland County: Bureau of Consumer Affairs, 35 E. High St., Carlisle, PA 17013

Delaware County: Office of Consumer Affairs, Toal Building, 2nd and Orange Sts., Media, Pa. 19063

Lancaster County: Consumer Protection Commission, Lancaster County Courthouse, Lancaster, PA 17602

Montgomery County: Consumer Affairs Department, County Courthouse, Norristown, PA 19404

Schuylkill County: Consumer Protection Agency, County Courthouse, Pottsville, PA 17901

Westmoreland County: Bureau of Consumer Affairs, 102 W. Otterman St., PO Box Q, Greensburg, PA 15601

York County: York County Consumer Protection Office, Courthouse, 28 E. Market St., York, PA 17401

CITY OFFICES

Philadelphia: Mayor's Office of Consumer Services, 143 City Hall, Philadelphia, PA 19107. Also, Economic Crime Unit, District Attorney's Office, Centre Square W., 16th and Market Sts., 24th floor, Philadelphia, PA 19102

RHODE ISLAND: None

SOUTH CAROLINA: None

SOUTH DAKOTA: None

TENNESSEE: No County Offices, One City Office

Nashville: Mayor's Office of Consumer Affairs, 107 Metro Courthouse, Nashville, TN 37201

TEXAS: 7 County Offices (for 11 counties), 3 City Offices

COUNTY OFFICES

Bexar County: Consumer Fraud Division, Office of Criminal District Attorney, San Antonio, TX 78205

Dallas County: Consumer Fraud Division, Special Crime Division, 2700 Stemmons Expressway, 500 Stemmons Tower East, Dallas, TX 75207

El Paso, Culberson, and Hudspeth Counties: Consumer Protection Division, Office of Attorney General, El Paso County Annex Building, 4824 Alberta St., Suite 160, El Paso, TX 79905

Harris County: Consumer Fraud Division, Office of District Attorney, 201 Fannin Bank Building, Houston, TX 77002

Tarrant County: Assistant District Attorney, Economic Crimes, 200 W. Belknap St., Fort Worth, TX 76102

Travis County: Consumer Coordinator, Consumer Affairs Office, 624B N. Pleasant Valley Road, Austin, TX 78702

Weller, Austin, and Fayette Counties: District Attorney, County Courthouse, Box 171, Hempstead, TX 77445

CITY OFFICES

Dallas: Department of Consumer Affairs, City Hall, Room 2BN, Dallas, TX 75201

Fort Worth: Office of Consumer Affairs, Weights and Measures, 1800 University Drive, Room 208, Fort Worth, TX 76107

San Antonio: Office of Consumer Services, Dept. of Human Services, 600 Hemisfair Way, Building 249, San Antonio, TX 78205

UTAH: None

VERMONT: None

VIRGINIA: 3 County Offices, 5 City Offices

COUNTY OFFICES

Arlington County: Office of Consumer Affairs, 2049 15th St. N., Arlington, VA 22201

Fairfax County: Department of Consumer Affairs, 4031 University Drive, Fairfax, VA 22030

Prince William County: Office of Consumer Affairs, 15960 Cardinal Drive, Woodbridge, VA 22191

CITY OFFICES

Alexandria: Consumer Affairs Coordinator, Office of Consumer Affairs, PO Box 178, City Hall, Alexandria, VA 22313

Newport News: Office of Consumer Affairs, City Hall, 2400 Washington Ave., Newport News, VA 23607

Norfolk: Division of Consumer Affairs, 804 City Hall Building, Norfolk, VA 23501

Roanoke: Consumer Protection Division, 353 Municipal Building, 215 Church Ave. SW, Roanoke, VA 24011

Virginia Beach: Division of Consumer Protection, City Hall, Virginia Beach, 23456

WASHINGTON: 1 County Office, 2 City Offices

COUNTY OFFICE

King County: Chief Deputy Prosecuting Attorney, Fraud Division, E531 King County Courthouse, Seattle, WA 98104

CITY OFFICES

Everett: Weights and Measures Department, City Hall, 3002 Wetmore Ave., Everett, WA 98201

Seattle: Department of Licenses and Consumer Affairs, 102 Municipal Building, Seattle, WA 98104

WEST VIRGINIA: No County Offices, One City Office

Charleston: Consumer Protection Department, PO Box 2749, Charleston, WV 25330

WISCONSIN: 5 County Offices, No City Offices

Kenosha County: Consumer Investigator, 912 56th St., Kenosha, WI 53140

Marathon County: District Attorney's Office, Marathon County Court House, Wausau, WI 54401

Milwaukee County: Assistant District Attorney, Consumer Fraud Unit, 821 W. State St., Room 412, Milwaukee, WI 53233

Portage County: District Attorney's Office, Consumer Fraud Unit, Portage County Court House, Stevens Point, WI 54481

Racine County: District Attorney's Office, Consumer Fraud Division, 730 Wisconsin Ave., Racine, WI 53403

WYOMING: None

F • Your State Consumer Protection Agency

The state consumer protection agencies are the spine of government efforts at consumer protection. The federal government, by and large, can police the marketplace for gross abuses, but in most cases isn't geared to act on individual complaints. Local governments and voluntary groups can do a lot. But unless they have strong help from state government, they will never be as effective as they otherwise could be. The state consumer protection agencies can coordinate local and voluntary efforts, press legislatures for strong consumer protection laws, and see that those laws are enforced. In so doing, the state agencies can set a tone for the marketplace, discouraging potential transgressors from shoddy dealing or deception. Most important, it is the state agencies that have the staff and the budget to handle individual consumer complaints in most areas.

The effectiveness of these agencies varies tremendously from state to state. It can even vary within a given state over time, depending on appointments made by the governor in power, and on the level of staffing and funding provided by the state legislature at a particular time.

Furthermore, the effectiveness of your state consumer protection agency depends, to some extent, on how you use it. The more clearly you document your complaint and the more persistently you follow up (within the limits of common courtesy), the better are the chances that your state consumer protection agency will be able to help you resolve a problem.

Most state consumer protection agencies now receive more than 3,000 complaints a year (250 a month). More than a third of the state consumer agencies process more than 12,000 complaints a year (1,000 a month). That's good and bad. It's good in that the staff develops specialized knowledge and experience. It's also good in that it shows the agencies fill a genuine need, and that the public is aware the agencies exist. It's bad in the sense that your complaint can get lost, or can become just part of someone's routine. So you must be assertive enough to follow up on your complaint with the state agency, just as you would with a private business.

Which are the best state consumer protection agencies, and which are the worst? That's a difficult question to answer with any precision. In early 1980, around the time this book went to press, the federal Office of Consumer Affairs released a study of "Consumer Complaint Handling in America." The study was conducted by a Washington D.C. consulting group called Technical Assistance Research Programs, Inc., or TARP for short. The TARP study named names when it evaluated the effectiveness of federal agencies, and some results of those evaluations are included in this book. The TARP researchers undoubtedly looked at the effectiveness of quite a few state agencies, too (exactly how many isn't made clear in the report). But these findings were presented only on an aggregate basis, not state by state. (The same practice was followed with local governmental organizations, voluntary groups, and private businesses.) Jusifying their silence, the researchers stated that their legal authority was limited, and also that the "policy of nonattribution was adopted to gain the cooperation of these complaint handlers." I have made a request for the detailed data under the Freedom of Information Act, but, as of the time this book went to press, have not succeeded in obtaining the data. If I do obtain it, it's possible the additional information will be in a subsequent edition of this book.

The only attempt I know of to obtain and publish comparative data on the effectiveness of state consumer protection departments was made in 1975, by me, in connection with an earlier version of this book (published in 1976 under the title *A Consumer's Arsenal*). I sent a questionnaire to consumer protection agencies in all fifty states and received, after considerable prodding, forty-five usable responses. The responses on two crucial questions are shown in the table below. Those questions were: (1) What percentage of cases are successfully resolved? (2) What is the average waiting time for a consumer needing aid?

Some limitations to my data should be noted. First, the data are now several years old. Second, my question about successful resolution should have been worded better, to clarify whether success was in the eyes of the agency or the consumer. Third, the answers represent the judgments or estimates (possibly self-serving) of agency personnel, with no independent verification of their accuracy.

Despite those sizable limitations, I think my survey still provides information of considerable interest to consumers. In addition to providing the basis for the table below, my 1975 survey also provides the basis for the Gripe Index (What Bothers Consumers Most?) shown in Appendix I.

SURVEY OF STATE CONSUMER PROTECTION AGENCIES

State Agency	*Percentage of Complaints Successfully Resolved*	*Average Waiting Time for Consumer*
Alabama Governor's Office of Consumer Protection	40%	4 weeks
Alaska Office of Attorney General Consumer Protection Section	NR	NR
Arizona Office of the Attorney General, Economic Protection Division	ND	6–8 weeks

SURVEY OF STATE CONSUMER PROTECTION AGENCIES

State Agency	*Percentage of Complaints Successfully Resolved*	*Average Waiting Time for Consumer*
Arkansas Attorney General's Office Consumer Protection Division	ND	ND
California Department of Consumer Affairs	ND	ND (F)
Colorado Office of Consumer Affairs	35–40% (A)	4 weeks
Connecticut Department of Consumer Protection	ND	3–5 weeks (B)
Delaware Division of Consumer Affairs	75%	ND
District of Columbia Office of Consumer Affairs	75%	1 week
Florida Fair Trade Practice Office, Department of Legal Affairs	ND	ND
Georgia Consumer Services Program	80%	1 week
Hawaii Office of Consumer Protection	85%	6–8 weeks
Idaho Office of Attorney General Consumer Protection Division	NR	NR
Illinois Office of the Attorney General, Consumer Fraud and Protection Division (Chicago)	65%	2–3 weeks
Consumer Protection Division (Springfield)	90%	4–5 weeks
Indiana Office of the Attorney General, Consumer Protection Division	ND	ND
Iowa Department of Justice Consumer Protection Division	70%	4–6 weeks

SURVEY OF STATE CONSUMER PROTECTION AGENCIES

State Agency	*Percentage of Complaints Successfully Resolved*	*Average Waiting Time for Consumer*
Kansas Office of Attorney General Consumer Protection Division	85%	2 weeks
Kentucky Office of Attorney General, Consumer Protection Division	70%	4 weeks (E)
Louisiana Governor's Office of Consumer Protection	75%	ND
Maine Office of Attorney General Division of Consumer Fraud and Protection	70%	ND
Maryland Office of Attorney General, Consumer Protection Division	ND	ND
Massachusetts Executive Office of Consumer Affairs, Consumer Complaint Division	95%	2 weeks
Michigan Consumer Council	60%	4 weeks
Michigan Office of Attorney General, Consumer Protection Division	50%	1½ weeks
Minnesota Office of Consumer Services	70%	5–6 weeks
Minnesota Office of Attorney General, Consumer Protection Division	85%	3 weeks
Mississippi Office of Attorney General, Consumer Protection Division	48%	4 weeks
Missouri Office of Attorney General, Consumer Protection Division	70–75%	1½ weeks

SURVEY OF STATE CONSUMER PROTECTION AGENCIES

State Agency	*Percentage of Complaints Successfully Resolved*	*Average Waiting Time for Consumer*
Montana Consumer Affairs Division, Department of Business Regulation	80%	2 weeks
Nebraska Department of Justice Consumer Protection Division	NR	NR
Nevada Consumer Affairs Division Department of Commerce	90% (C)	1–2 weeks
New Hampshire Office of Attorney General, Consumer Protection Division	75% (A)	4–8 weeks
New Jersey Office of Consumer Affairs	60% (A)	2–4 weeks
New Mexico Office of Attorney General, Consumer Protection Division	61%	19 weeks
New York Office of Attorney General, Consumer Frauds and Protection Bureau	ND	ND
North Carolina Office of Attorney General, Consumer Protection Division	65–70%	4–8 weeks
North Dakota Office of Attorney General, Consumer Fraud Division	97%	5 weeks
Ohio Office of Attorney General Consumer Frauds and Crimes Section	ND	2–3 weeks
Oklahoma Office of Attorney General	51% (A)	ND
Oregon Office of Attorney General Consumer Protection Division	63% (C)	ND

F • Your State Consumer Protection Agency

SURVEY OF STATE CONSUMER PROTECTION AGENCIES

State Agency	*Percentage of Complaints Successfully Resolved*	*Average Waiting Time for Consumer*
Pennsylvania Office of Attorney General, Bureau of Consumer Protection	50–75%	ND
Rhode Island Office of Attorney General, Consumer Affairs Division	90%	1 week
South Carolina Department of Consumer Affairs	45%	1 week (D)
South Dakota Division of Consumer Protection, Department of Commerce and Consumer Affairs	ND	1 week
Tennessee Office of Attorney General, Consumer Protection Coordinator	20%	3–4 weeks
Texas Office of Attorney General Antitrust and Consumer Protection Division	75%	4 weeks
Utah Office of Attorney General Consumer Protection Division	55%	3 weeks
Vermont Office of Attorney General, Consumer Fraud Division	60–70%	1 week
Virginia Office of Consumer Affairs Department of Agriculture and Commerce	50–60%	ND
Washington Office of Attorney General, Consumer Protection and Antitrust Division	NR	NR
West Virginia Office of Attorney General, Consumer Protection Division	55–60% (A)	4 weeks

SURVEY OF STATE CONSUMER PROTECTION AGENCIES

State Agency	*Percentage of Complaints Successfully Resolved*	*Average Waiting Time for Consumer*
Wisconsin Department of Justice Office of Consumer Protection	50%	4–6 weeks
Wyoming Office of Attorney General, Consumer Affairs Division	75%	3–4 weeks

NR No reply to two letters and two or more telephone calls.
ND No data available.
A Figure refers to percentage of complaints resolved in favor of consumer.
B Figure refers to waiting time before investigation *begins.*
C Figure refers to percentage of complaints resolved to satisfaction of agency, not to satisfaction of consumer.
D More recent reports furnished to the National Association of Consumer Agency Administrators (NACAA) suggest the current average waiting time is about 4 weeks.
E More recent reports furnished to NACAA suggest the current average waiting time is about 3 weeks.
F More recent reports furnished to NACAA suggest the current average waiting time is about 6–7 weeks.

This chart isn't gospel, by any means. It does, however, suggest the heights of effectiveness to which some consumer protection agencies (at least by their own account) may rise, and the depths to which others may sink.

The best way for you to determine the effectiveness of these agencies is to give them a try. Many states now have more than one state agency that handles a variety of complaints. So you may have recourses not even mentioned in the chart above. When there's more than one state consumer protection agency, you can contact them simultaneously or sequentially, depending on your preferences and the strategy you want to follow in a particular dispute.

If you get into a dispute with an out-of-state firm, keep in mind that you may be able to use the consumer protection agency in the firm's home state as a recourse for resolving the dispute. I know of no case in which a consumer protection agency refused to handle a case because the complainant wasn't a state resident.

Addresses of the state consumer protection agencies, listed alphabetically by state, are below.

Alabama

- Governor's Office of Consumer Protection, 138 Adams Ave., Montgomery, AL 36130 (Toll-free number: 800-392-5658)
- Consumer Services Director, Office of Attorney General, 669 S. Lawrence St., Montgomery, AL 36104

Alaska

- Consumer Protection Section, Office of Attorney General, 420 L Street, Suite 100, Anchorage, AK 99501

  Branch Offices: (1) State Court Office Building, 604 Barnette, Room 228, Fairbanks, AK 99707; (2) Pouch K, Room 1568, State Capitol, Juneau, AK 99811

Arizona

- Financial Fraud Division, 207 State Capitol Building, Phoenix, AZ 85007

  Branch Office: Economic Protection Division, 100 N. Stone Ave., Suite 1004, Tucson, AZ 85701

Arkansas

- Consumer Protection Division, Office of Attorney General, Justice Building, Little Rock, AR 72201 (Toll-free number: 800-482-8982, in Arkansas only)

California

- California Department of Consumer Affairs, 1020 N Street, Sacramento, CA 95814 (Toll-free number for auto repair complaints only: 800-366-5131, in California only)
  Branch offices: (1) 107 S. Broadway, Room 8020, Los Angeles, CA 90012 (2) 30 Van Ness Ave., Room 2100, San Francisco, CA 94102
- Public Inquiry Unit, Office of Attorney General, 555 Capitol Mall, Sacramento, CA 95814

Colorado

- Consumer Section, Office of Attorney General, 1525 Sherman St., 4th floor, Denver, CO 80203
- Consumer and Food Specialist, Colorado Department of Agriculture, 1525 Sherman St., Denver, CO 80203

Connecticut

- Department of Consumer Protection, State Office Building, Hartford, CN 06115 (Toll-free number: 800-842-2649, in Connecticut only)

Delaware

- Consumer Affairs Division, Department of Community Affairs and Economic Development, 820 N. French St., 4th floor, Wilmington, DE 19801
- Consumer Protection Division, Department of Justice, 820 N. French St., Wilmington, DE 19801

District of Columbia

- D.C. Office of Consumer Protection, 1424 K Street NW, Washington DC 20005

Florida

- Division of Consumer Services, 110 Mayo Building, Tallahassee, FL 32304 (Toll-free number: 800-342-2176, in Florida only)
- Consumer Protection and Fair Trade Practices Bureau,

Department of Legal Affairs, State Capitol, Tallahassee, FL 32304

Branch Offices: (1) Dade County Regional Service Center, 401 NW 2d Ave., Suite 820, Miami, FL 33128; (2) 1313 Tampa St., 8th floor, Park Trammell, Tampa, FL 33602

Georgia

- Governor's Office of Consumer Affairs, 225 Peachtree St. NE, Suite 400, Atlanta, GA 30303 (Toll-free number: 800-282-4900)
- Attorney General for Deceptive Practices, Office of Attorney General, 132 State Judicial Building, Atlanta, GA 30334

Hawaii

- Director of Consumer Protection, Office of the Governor, 250 S. King St., PO Box 3767, Honolulu, HI 96811 (Toll-free number for complaints: 800-548-2540)

Idaho

- Consumer Protection Division, Office of Attorney General, State Capitol, Boise, ID 83720 (Toll-free number: 800-632-5937)

Illinois

- Special Assistant to the Governor, Consumer Advocate Office, Office of the Governor, 160 N. LaSalle St., Room 2010, Chicago, IL 60601
- Consumer Fraud Section, Office of Attorney General, 228 N. LaSalle St., Room 1242, Chicago, IL 60601

  Branch offices: (1) 2151 Madison, Bellwood, IL 60104; (2) 50 Raupp Blvd., Buffalo Grove, IL 60090; (3) 1104 N. Ashland Ave., Chicago, IL 60622; (4) 13051 Grainwood Ave., Blue Island, IL 60406; (5) 4750 N. Broadway, Room 216, Chicago, IL 60640; (6)

7906 S. Cottage Grove, Chicago, IL 60619; (7) 800 Lee St., Des Plaines, IL 60016, Saturday only; (8) Evanston Library, 1703 Orrington, Evanston, IL 60204, Saturday only; (9) PO Box 752, 71 N. Ottawa St., Joliet, IL 60434; (10) 6250 N. Lincoln Ave., Morton Grove, IL 60050, Saturday only; (11) 163 Lakehurst, Waukegan, IL 60085, Saturday only; (12) 1000 Schaumberg Road, Schaumberg, IL 60172; (13) 5127 Oakton St., Skokie, IL 60077; 500 S. Second St., Springfield, IL 62706; (14) 103 S. Washington, Suite 12, Carbondale, IL 62901; (15) 818 Martin Luther King Drive, St. Louis, IL 62201; (16) 500 Main St., Peoria, IL 61602; (17) 208 18th St., Rock Island, IL 61201; (19) 301 Rockriver Savings Building, Rockford, IL 61101

Indiana

- Consumer Protection Division, Office of Attorney General, 215 State House, Indianapolis, IN 46204 (Toll-free number: 800-382-5516)

Iowa

- Consumer Protection Division, Office of Attorney General, 1300 E. Walnut, Des Moines, IA 50319
- Citizens' Aid Ombudsman, 515 E. 12th St., Des Moines, IA 50319

Kansas

- Consumer Protection Division, Office of Attorney General, Kansas Judicial Center, 301 W. 10th, 2d floor, Topeka, KS 66612

Kentucky

- Consumer Protection Division, Office of Attorney General, Executive Building, 209 St. Clair St., Frankfort, KY 40601 (Toll-free number: 800-372-2960)

Louisiana

- State Office of Consumer Protection, PO Box 44091, Suite 1218, Capitol Station, Baton Rouge, LA 70804 (Toll-free number: 800-272-9868)
- Consumer Protection Section, Office of Attorney General, 1885 Wooddale Blvd., Suite 1208, Baton Rouge, LA 70806

  Branch office: 234 Loyola Ave., 7th floor, New Orleans, LA 70112
- Bureau of Marketing, Department of Agriculture, PO Box 44184, Capitol Station, Baton Rouge, LA 70804

Maine

- Consumer and Antitrust Division, Office of Attorney General, 505 State Office Building, Augusta, ME 04333
- Bureau of Consumer Protection, State House Station 35, Augusta, ME 04333

Maryland

- Consumer Protection Division, Office of Attorney General, 131 E. Redwood St., Baltimore, MD 21202

Massachusetts

- Executive Office of Consumer Affairs, John W. McCormack Building, One Ashburton Place, Room 1411, Boston, MA 02108
- Consumer Protection Division, Department of Attorney General, One Ashburton Place, 19th floor, Boston, MA 02108

  Branch office: 235 Chestnut St., Springfield, MA 01103
- Massachusetts Consumers' Council, 100 Cambridge St., Room 2109, Boston, MA 02202

Michigan

- Consumer Protection Division, Office of Attorney General, 690 Law Building, Lansing, MI 48913

- Michigan Consumers Council, 414 Hollister Building, 106 N. Allegan St., Lansing, MI 48933 (Toll-free number: 800-292-5680)

Minnesota

- Consumer Protection Division, Office of Attorney General, 102 State Capitol, St. Paul, MN 55155
- Office of Consumer Services, 7th and Roberts Sts., St. Paul, MN 55101

  Branch office: 604 Alworth Building, Duluth, MN 55802

Mississippi

- Consumer Protection Division, Office of Attorney General, Justice Building, PO Box 220, Jackson, MS 39205
- Consumer Protection Division, Department of Agriculture and Commerce, High and President Sts., PO Box 1609, Jackson, MS 39205

Missouri

- Consumer Protection Division, Office of Attorney General, Supreme Court Building, PO Box 899, Jefferson City, MO 65102

  Branch offices: (1) 705 Olive St., Suite 1323, St. Louis, MO 63101; 615 E. 13th St., Kansas City, MO 64106
- Missouri Consumer Information Center, PO Box 1157, Jefferson City, MO 65102

  Branch offices: (1) 615 E. 13th St., Kansas City, MO 64106; (2) 330 Mansion House Center, St. Louis, MO 63102

Montana

- Consumer Affairs Division, Department of Business Regulation, 805 N. Main St., Helena, MT 59601

Nebraska

- Consumer Protection Division, Office of Attorney General, State House, Lincoln, NB 68509
- Consumer Consultant, Department of Agriculture, 301 Centennial Mall South, PO Box 94947, Lincoln, NB 68509

Nevada

- Consumer Affairs Division, Office of Attorney General, 2501 E. Sahara Ave., 3d floor, Las Vegas, NV 89158
- Consumer Affairs Division, Department of Commerce, 201 Nye Building, Capitol Complex, Carson City, NV 89710 (Toll-free number: 800-992-0973)

New Hampshire

- Consumer Protection and Antitrust Division, Office of Attorney General, State House Annex, Concord, NH 03301

New Jersey

- Division of Consumer Affairs, Department of Law and Public Safety, 1100 Raymond Blvd., Room 504, Newark, NJ 07102
- Department of Public Advocate, PO Box 141, Trenton, NJ 08625 (Handles complaints against state agencies only; toll-free number: 800-792-8600)
- Division of Consumer Complaints, Legal and Economic Research, PO Box CN040, Trenton, NJ 08625

New Mexico

- Consumer and Economic Crime Division, Office of Attorney General, PO Box 1508, Santa Fe, NM 87501

New York

- Consumer Frauds and Protection Bureau, Office of Attorney General: Two World Trade Center, New York, NY 10047 *or* State Capitol, Albany, NY 12224

Branch offices: (1) 10 Lower Metcalf Plaza, Auburn, NY 13021; (2) 44 Hawley St., State Office Building, Binghamton, NY 13901; (3) 65 Court St., Buffalo, NY 14202; (4) Suffolk State Office Building, Veterans Memorial Highway, Hauppauge, NY 11787; (5) 48 Cornelia St., Plattsburgh, NY 12901; (6) 65 Broad St., Rochester, NY 14614; (7) 333 E. Washington St., Syracuse, NY 13202; (8) 40 Garden St., Poughkeepsie, NY 12601; (9) 207 Genesee St., Box 528, Utica, NY 13501; (10) 317 Washington St.,Watertown, NY 13601

- Consumer Protection Board, 99 Washington Ave., Albany, NY 12210

  Branch office: Two World Trade Center, Room 8225, 82d floor, New York, NY 10047

North Carolina

- Consumer Protection Division, Office of Attorney General, Justice Building, PO Box 629, Raleigh, NC 27602
- Office of Consumer Services, Department of Agriculture, PO Box 27647, Raleigh, NC 27611

North Dakota

- Consumer Fraud Division, Office of Attorney General, State Capitol Building, Bismarck, ND 58505 (Toll-free number for North Dakota residents only: 800-472-2600)
- Consumer Affairs Office, State Laboratories Department, Box 937, Bismarck, ND 58505 (Toll-free number for North Dakota residents only: 800-472-2927)

Ohio

- Consumer Frauds and Crimes Section, Office of Attorney General, 30 E. Broad St., Columbus, OH 43215

Oklahoma

- Department of Consumer Affairs, 460 Jim Thorpe Building, Oklahoma City, OK 73105

- Assistant Attorney General for Consumer Protection, 112 State Capitol Building, Oklahoma City, OK 73105

Oregon

- Consumer Protection Division, Office of Attorney General, 520 SW Yamhill St., Portland, OR 97204
- Consumer Services Division, Department of Commerce, Labor and Industries Building, Salem, OR 97310

Pennsylvania

- Bureau of Consumer Protection, Department of Justice, 301 Market St., 9th floor, Harrisburg, PA 17101

  Branch offices: (1) 133 N. 5th St., Allentown, PA 18102; (2) 919 State Street, Room 203, Erie, PA 16501; (3) 1405 Locust St., Suite 825, Philadelphia, PA 19102; (4) 300 Liberty Ave., Room 1405, Pittsburgh, PA 15222; (5) 100 Lackawanna Ave., 105A State Office Building, Scranton, PA 18503
- Rural Coordinator, Pennsylvania Department of Agriculture, 615 Howard Ave., Altoona, PA 16601
- Consumer Advocate, Department of Justice, Strawberry Square, 14th floor, Harrisburg, PA 17127

Rhode Island

- Public Protection Consumer Unit, Department of Attorney General, 56 Pine St., Providence, RI 02903

South Carolina

- Office of Citizens Service, Governor's Office, PO Box 11450, Columbia, SC 29211
- Department of Consumer Affairs, 2221 Devine St., Columbia, SC 29211 (Toll-free number: 800-922-1594)
- Assistant Attorney General for Consumer Protection, 2303 Devine St., Columbia, SC 29205
- State Ombudsman, Office of Executive Policy and Program, 1205 Pendleton St., 4th floor, Columbia, SC 29201

South Dakota

- Division of Consumer Protection, Office of Attorney General, Capitol Building, Pierre, SD 57501

  Branch office: 114 S. Main Ave., Sioux Falls, SD 57102

Tennessee

- Division of Consumer Affairs, Department of Agriculture, Ellington Agriculture Center, Box 40627, Melrose Station, Nashville, TN 37204 (Toll-free number: 800-342-8385)
- Assistant Attorney General for Consumer Protection, 450 James Robertson Parkway, Nashville, TN 37219

Texas

- Consumer Protection and Antitrust Division, Office of Attorney General, PO Box 12548, Capitol Station, Austin, TX 78711

  Branch offices: (1) 4313 N. 10th, Suite F, McAllen, TX 78501; (2) 701 Commerce, Suite 200, Dallas, TX 75202; (3) 4824 Alberta Ave., Suite 160, El Paso, TX 79905; (4) 312 County Office Building, 806 Broadway, Lubbock, TX 79401; (5) 200 Main Plaza, Suite 400, San Antonio, TX 78205; (6) 723 Main St., Suite 610, Houston, TX 77002; (7) 201 E. Belknap St., Fort Worth, TX 76102

Utah

- Division of Consumer Affairs, Utah Trade Commission, Department of Business Regulation, 330 E. Fourth St., Salt Lake City, UT 84111
- Consumer Protection Unit, Office of Attorney General, 236 State Capitol, Salt Lake City, UT 84114

Vermont

- Consumer Protection Division, Office of Attorney General, 109 State St., Montpelier, VT 05602 (Toll-free number: 800-642-5149)

Virginia

- Division of Consumer Council, Office of Attorney General, 11 S. 12th St., Suite 308, Richmond, VA 23219
- State Office of Consumer Affairs, Department of Agriculture and Consumer Services, 825 E. Broad St., Box 1163, Richmond, VA 23209 (Toll-free number for complaints regarding state agencies: 800-552-9963)

Washington

- Consumer Protection and Antitrust Division, Office of Attorney General, 1366 Dexter Horton Building, Seattle, WA 98104 (Toll-free number: 800-552-0700)

  Branch offices: (1) Temple of Justice, Olympia, WA 98504; (2) 960 Paulsen Professional Building, Spokane, WA 99201; (3) 620 Perkins Building, Tacoma, WA 98402; (4) 215 Union Ave. Building, Olympia, WA 98504

West Virginia

- Consumer Protection Division, Office of Attorney General, 3412 Staunton Ave. SE, Charleston, WV 25305
- Consumer Protection Division, Department of Labor, 1900 Washington St. E., Charleston, WV 25305 (Handles complaints regarding weights and measures, bedding and upholstery)

Wisconsin

- Office of Consumer Protection, Department of Justice, State Capitol, Madison, WI 53702

  Branch office: Milwaukee State Office Building, 819 N. 6th St., Room 520, Milwaukee, WI 53203
- Division of Consumer Protection, Department of Agriculture, Trade and Consumer Protection, PO Box 8911,

Madison, WI 53708 (Toll-free number: 800-362-8025 in Wisconsin only)

Branch offices: (1) 1727 Loring St., Altoona, WI 54720; (2) 1181 A Western Ave., Green Bay, WI 54303; (3) 10320 W. Silver Spring Drive, Milwaukee, WI 53225

Wyoming

- Assistant Attorney General for Consumer Protection, 123 Capitol Building, Cheyenne, WY 82002

G • Federal Referral Centers

If you're stumped about where to go with a complaint, first check Part I of this book, which describes avenues worth pursuing for dozens of common consumer complaints. If you're still in doubt, you might get some guidance from the federal government.

As of early 1980, thirty-six states, plus the District of Columbia, have Federal Information Centers, whose staffers are trained to refer you to the appropriate federal agency (or, in some cases, to state or local agencies). These centers are not exclusively designed for complaint handling; they can also be of use when you simply want information on some topic. Phone charges for calling the centers are usually small, since in many cases a local call will connect you with a toll-free tieline to a distant center. In the list below, compiled by the federal Office of Consumer Affairs, italicized entries refer to such tielines. Entries in regular type refer to the centers themselves. If you prefer to visit a center, rather than call, you can get the address from a telephone directory or by calling ahead.

Phone numbers for Federal Information Centers are as follows.

ALABAMA
Birmingham *205-322-8591*
Mobile *205-438-1421*

ARIZONA
Phoenix 602-261-3313
Tucson *602-622-1511*

ARKANSAS
Little Rock *501-378-6177*

CALIFORNIA
Los Angeles 213-688-3800
Sacramento 916-440-3344
San Diego 714-293-6030
San Francisco 415-556-6600
San Jose *408-275-7422*
Santa Ana *714-836-2386*

COLORADO
Colorado Springs *303-471-9491*
Denver 303-837-3602
Pueblo *303-544-9523*

CONNECTICUT
Hartford *203-527-2617*
New Haven *203-624-4720*

DISTRICT OF COLUMBIA
Washington 202-755-8660

FLORIDA
Fort Lauderdale *305-522-8531*
Jacksonville *904-354-4756*
Miami 305-350-4155
Orlando *305-422-1800*
St. Petersburg 813-893-3495
Tampa *813-229-7911*
West Palm Beach *305-833-7566*

GEORGIA
Atlanta 404-221-6891

HAWAII
Honolulu 808-546-8620

ILLINOIS
Chicago 312-353-4242

INDIANA
Gary/ Hammond *219-883-4110*
Indianapolis 317-269-7373

IOWA
Des Moines *515-284-4448*

KANSAS
Topeka *913-295-2866*
Wichita *316-263-6931*

KENTUCKY
Louisville 502-582-6261

LOUISIANA
New Orleans 504-589-6696

MARYLAND
Baltimore 301-962-4980

MASSACHUSETTS
Boston 617-223-7121

MICHIGAN
Detroit 313-226-7016
Grand Rapids *616-451-2628*

MINNESOTA
Minneapolis 612-725-2073

MISSOURI
Kansas City 816-374-2466
St. Joseph 816-233-8206
St. Louis 314-425-4106

NEBRASKA
Omaha 402-221-3353

NEW JERSEY
Newark 201-645-3600
Paterson/Passaic 201-523-0717
Trenton 609-396-4400

NEW MEXICO
Albuquerque 505-766-3091
Santa Fe 505-983-7743

NEW YORK
Albany 518-463-4421
Buffalo 716-846-4010
New York 212-264-4464
Rochester 716-546-5075
Syracuse 315-476-8545

NORTH CAROLINA
Charlotte 704-376-3600

OHIO
Akron 216-375-5638
Cincinnati 513-684-2801
Cleveland 216-522-4040
Columbus 614-221-1014
Dayton 513-223-7377
Toledo 419-241-3223

OKLAHOMA
Oklahoma City 405-231-4868
Tulsa 918-584-4193

OREGON
Portland 503-221-2222

PENNSYLVANIA
Allentown/Bethlehem 215-821-7785
Philadelphia 215-597-7042
Pittsburgh 412-644-3456
Scranton 717-346-7081

RHODE ISLAND
Providence 401-331-5565

TENNESSEE
Chattanooga 615-265-8231
Memphis 901-521-3285
Nashville 615-242-5056

TEXAS
Austin 512-472-5494
Dallas 214-767-8585
Fort Worth 817-334-3624
Houston 713-226-5711
San Antonio 512-224-4471

UTAH
Ogden 801-399-1347
Salt Lake City 801-524-5353

VIRGINIA
Newport News 804-244-0480
Norfolk 804-441-3101
Richmond 804-643-4928
Roanoke 703-982-8591

WASHINGTON		WISCONSIN	
Seattle	206-442-0570	*Milwaukee*	*414-271-2273*
Tacoma	*206-383-5230*		

The federal Office of Consumer Affairs (OCA) may also serve as a referral center of last resort. The OCA used to encourage consumers to write to it. Though OCA didn't handle many complaints itself, its staff was expert at forwarding complaints to the appropriate agencies. Now OCA is trying to get out of the complaint-handling business. To this end, it has published a useful seventy-seven page booklet called *Consumer's Resource Handbook.* The idea is to inform consumers where they can take complaints, thus getting OCA out from the middle. A great deal of the information in the OCA booklet—but not all of it—is found in this book. You may wish to send for the booklet, by writing the Consumer Information Center, Dept. 532 G, Pueblo, CO 81009. Single copies are free.

If you've called a Federal Information Center, read this book and the OCA booklet, and *still* don't know where to turn for help, you can try writing to the U.S. Office of Consumer Affairs, Washington DC 20201.

H • The Federal Trade Commission— A Consumers' Watchdog

Starting in 1979, the Federal Trade Commission has become something of a political football, which business lobbyists and politicians have been kicking around with great force. How *dare* the FTC meddle with the right of children to eat presweetened breakfast cereals, or to watch toy commercials on their favorite television shows? How *dare* the FTC insinuate that cash-value life insurance policies may be poor investments, or that funeral parlors may not have the best interests of their clients at heart? Who does the FTC think it is—Big Brother?

So goes the refrain. And to this tune, sad to say, efforts have been made on Capitol Hill to cut back the FTC's funding and to prohibit the FTC from investigating certain types of businesses. There have also been attempts to take away the FTC's power to issue "trade regulation rules" prescribing certain standards of conduct for particular industries. The outcome of these power struggles was unclear as this book went to press in 1980.

I think that the FTC over the past decade has acted, on the whole, forcefully, openly, and responsively in defending consumer interests. By and large, I don't think it has tended to impose red tape or excessive costs on the industries it regulates. By and large, I think it has done a good job of trying to make the marketplace a place where the consumer has a fair shake. Whether the FTC will continue to be effective into the 1980s remains to be seen. But it behooves consumers to understand that the Federal Trade Commission is the closest thing to a national consumer protection agency we have.

Being national in scope, the FTC can't always respond quickly—or even at all—to individual complaints. Sometimes it stockpiles complaints, and takes action only when a large number of complaints are received against a particular company or industry.

In some cases, though, you will get help on your individual complaint from the FTC. It depends what the subject of your complaint is, and what the staff situation is at a particular FTC office at a particular time. You're especially likely to get action if your complaint is in an area where the FTC has specific statutory authority (e.g., advertising, antitrust, clothing labeling) or if it's in an area the FTC has been investigating (e.g., health spas, hearing aids, funeral parlors).

In any case, I'd try the regional office of the FTC on most complaints if your letters to the seller or manufacturer, and to local or state authorities, haven't resolved the dispute. At best, you'll get help for yourself. At worst, your complaint will go on file and might eventually help someone else.

The FTC's national headquarters address is simply Federal Trade Commission, Washington DC 20580. For most complaints, write to the regional office nearest you. Addresses of the regional offices are as follows.

- *Atlanta:* Room 1000, 1718 Peachtree St. NW, Atlanta, GA 30309
- *Boston:* Room 1301, 150 Causeway St., Boston, MA 02114
- *Chicago:* Suite 1437, 55 East Monroe St., Chicago, IL 60603
- *Cleveland:* Suite 500, Mall Building, 118 St. Clair Ave., Cleveland, OH 44144
- *Dallas:* Suite 2665, 2001 Bryan St., Dallas, TX 75201
- *Denver:* Suite 2900, 1405 Curtis St., Denver, CO 80202
- *Los Angeles:* Room 13209, Federal Building, 11000 Wilshire Blvd., Los Angeles, CA 90024
- *New York:* 2243-EB, Federal Building, 26 Federal Plaza, New York, NY 10007
- *San Francisco:* 450 Golden Gate Ave., Box 36005, San Francisco, CA 94102
- *Seattle:* 28th floor, Federal Building, 915 Second Ave., Seattle, WA 98174

I • The Food and Drug Administration

The importance of the FDA to consumers is almost impossible to overestimate. It's responsible for keeping off the market any drugs, food products, medical devices, or cosmetics that may be hazardous to people's health. To do this, it relies in part on citizen complaints.

Will the FDA get your money back for you? Probably not, at least not through direct intervention on your behalf. "We don't get involved in getting consumers' money back," an FDA spokesperson said. "But their complaints help us do our job properly." Your complaint to the FDA about a food, drug, medical device, or cosmetic could save another consumer from injury.

Indirectly, complaining to the FDA might also help you get your money back. Your complaint letter demonstrates your seriousness. Should the occasion arise, such a letter could also be evidence in small claims court, or in a conventional court. If the FDA takes action against a firm, that action could also be used as evidence. Naturally, you hope you won't have to go to court to get restitution, but if a company can see that you have a strong case, it's likely to settle a dispute without a court proceeding.

Like the Federal Trade Commission, though to a lesser extent, the FDA has become the center of political controversy. Its critics charge that it imposes excessive red tape on drug companies and medical practitioners; that it takes too long to approve new, experimental drugs; and that it tries too hard to protect Americans from themselves by regulating or banning substances not conclusively proved to be harmful. (In this last category of complaints, the chief bone of contention has been saccharin, though there have been many others, including the controversial so-called cancer drug, laetrile.)

There is probably some substance to the criticism about red tape. In my opinion, though, most of the criticisms of FDA are poorly founded. They reflect, I think, either a seeking for political advantage or an ignorance of proper drug-testing procedures in general and testing for carcinogenicity in particular.

The allegation that the FDA goes too far in trying to protect people from potential cancer-causing agents seems to me particularly uninformed. In fact, the FDA allows the presence of known or suspected cancer-causing agents in certain drugs when no better alternative is available. It does not allow the presence of such agents in food or cosmetics—and that, I believe, is exactly as it should be.

My point in defending the FDA here is that I think the agency has done, by and large, a good job. For it to continue doing so, it needs to be kept informed of problems in the marketplace it regulates.

Often complaints to the FDA involve emergencies: contaminated food, for example, can seriously affect the public health. That's one reason why the FDA has specific guidelines for complaints. "Give your name, address, telephone number, and directions on how to get to your home or place of business. State clearly what appears to be wrong. Describe in as much detail as possible the label of the product. Give any code marks that appear on the container. . . . Give the name and address of the store where the article was bought, and the date of purchase. Save whatever remains of the suspect product or the empty container for your doctor's guidance or possible examination by FDA. Retain any unopened containers of the product you bought at the same time. If any injury is involved, see your physician at once. Report the suspect product to the manufacturer, packer, or distributor shown on the label, and to the store where you bought it [as well as to FDA]."

You can send your complaint to FDA national headquarters if you wish (Director of Consumer Communications, HFJ-10, FDA, 5600 Fishers Lane, Rockville, MD 20852). But you might get faster action if you use one of the agency's thirty-two regional consumer affairs offices. They are listed, alphabetically by city, below.

- *Albany:* Clinton and Pearl Sts., Albany, NY 12207
- *Atlanta:* 800 W. Peachtree St. NW, Atlanta, GA 30309
- *Baltimore:* 900 Madison Ave., Baltimore, MD 21201
- *Boston:* 585 Commercial St., Boston, MA 02109
- *Buffalo:* 599 Delaware Ave., Buffalo, NY 14202
- *Chicago:* 1222 Main Post Office Building, Chicago, IL 60607
- *Chicago:* 175 W. Jackson Blvd., Chicago, IL 60604
- *Cincinnati:* 1141 Central Parkway, Cincinnati, OH 45202
- *Cleveland:* 601 Rockwell Ave., Cleveland, OH 44114
- *Dallas:* 500 S. Ervay St., Dallas, TX 75201
- *Denver:* 19th and California Sts., Denver, CO 80202
- *Detroit:* 1560 E. Jefferson Ave., Detroit, MI 48207
- *East Orange:* 20 Evergreen Place, East Orange, NJ 07018
- *Falls Church:* 701 W. Broad St., Falls Church, VA 22046
- *Grand Rapids:* 110 Michigan NW, Grand Rapids, MI 49502
- *Indianapolis:* 575 N. Pennsylvania, Indianapolis, IN 46204
- *Kansas City:* 1009 Cherry St., Kansas City, MO 64106
- *Los Angeles:* 1521 W. Pico Blvd., Los Angeles, CA 90015
- *Minneapolis:* 240 Hennepin Ave., Minneapolis, MN 55401
- *Nashville:* 297 Plus Park Blvd., Nashville, TN 37217
- *New Orleans:* 4229 Elysiana Field Ave., New Orleans, LA 70130
- *New York:* 850 3rd Ave., Brooklyn, NY 11232

- *Omaha:* 1619 Howard St., Omaha, NB 68102
- *Orlando:* PO Box 118, Orlando, FL 32802
- *Philadelphia:* 2nd and Chestnut Sts., Philadelphia, PA 19106
- *Pittsburgh:* 3 Parkway Center, Pittsburgh, PA 15220
- *Richmond:* 7th and Marshall Sts., Richmond, VA 23240
- *San Antonio:* 419 S. Main, San Antonio, TX 78204
- *San Francisco:* 50 United Nations Plaza, San Francisco, CA 94102
- *San Juan:* PO Box 4427, Old San Juan Station, San Juan, PR 00905
- *Seattle:* 909 1st Ave., Seattle, WA 98174
- *St. Louis:* 1114 Market St., St. Louis, MO 63101

J • The Consumer Product Safety Commission

If you spot a safety-related defect in any product (except food, drugs, medical devices, or cosmetics), the Consumer Product Safety Commission (CPSC) is the right federal agency to contact.

The CPSC won't help you get your money back. For that, you'll have to resort to complaint letters (see II-B), small claims court (II-N), a local or state consumer protection agency (II-E, II-F), or one of the other means described in this book.

Like the FDA, the CPSC may not bring you any monetary satisfaction, at least not directly, but it may bring you some emotional satisfaction. If there's an unsafe product on the market and if you can help get it off the market, you may be doing a lot of people a favor. You may even save someone from death or serious injury.

Here's how the CPSC works, according to a spokesperson: "When we have an indication of a defect, we go to the company involved. The company can propose voluntary corrective action, such as making a design change, and repurchasing the units that are already on the market. We monitor the corrective action. If we're not satisfied with it, we can conduct hearings and then order a recall and a correction. If other products of the same type are affected by the same hazard, then we put out a public request inviting interested parties to develop safety standards for that type of product. Of course, we have the last word on what standards are developed."

The CPSC has had a hand in several changes I applaud, such as the development of childproof caps for aspirin and other medications, and the drafting of standards specifying how close together crib slats should be. Those two measures have saved the lives of a lot of children and infants.

On the other hand, there's one thing about the CPSC that gets my goat. It's an attitude of, "File that complaint. If we get a lot of complaints against the same product or manufacturer, then we'll do something." I grant that a lot of federal agencies operate this way. You could even argue that they should operate this way, to set priorities for the use of limited funds and manpower. I can buy this argument for most agencies. But when an agency is dealing in safety matters, it doesn't seem right. As an example, I once bought a toy mop for my daughter, who happens to be more gentle on toys than most kids are. Within a day, the mop head fell off, revealing a long, sharply pointed piece of metal. Any toy constructed that way is in obvious violation of the CPSC's own guidelines for toy safety. So I called and wrote the agency. In due course, I received a letter saying the complaint had been filed, and the company would be investigated if enough complaints were received. I protested; the agency reaffirmed its policy.

I don't think this incident should discourage you from taking a complaint to the CPSC. After all, your complaint might be the one that pushes things over the critical threshold.

The CPSC makes it commendably easy for you to contact

them. You can call, toll-free, 800-638-8326. If you live in Maryland, it's 800-492-8363. If you're in Alaska or Hawaii (or Puerto Rico or the Virgin Islands) it's 800-638-8333. If you prefer to write, the address is Director, Office of Communications, Consumer Product Safety Commission, Washington DC 20207. Or you can contact one of the CPSC's thirteen regional offices. They're listed below, in alphabetical order by city.

- *Atlanta:* 1330 W. Peachtree St. NW, Atlanta, GA 30309
- *Boston:* 100 Summer St., 16th floor, Room 1607, Boston, MA 02110
- *Chicago:* 230 S. Dearborn St., Room 2945, Chicago, IL 60604
- *Cleveland:* Plaza 9 Building, Suite 520, 55 Erieview Plaza, 5th floor, Cleveland, OH 44114
- *Dallas:* 500 S. Ervay, Room 410C, Dallas, TX 75201
- *Denver:* Guaranty Bank Building, Suite 938, 817 17th St., Denver, CO 80202
- *Kansas City:* Traders National Bank Building, Suite 1500, 1125 Grand Ave., Kansas City, MO 64106
- *Los Angeles:* 3660 Wilshire Blvd., Suite 1100, Los Angeles, CA 90010
- *New York:* 6 World Trade Center, Vesey Street, 6th floor, New York, NY 10048
- *Philadelphia:* 400 Market St., 10th floor, Philadelphia, PA 19106
- *Saint Paul:* Metro Square, Suite 580, 7th and Robert, St. Paul, MN 55101
- *San Francisco:* 100 Pine St., Suite 500, San Francisco, CA 94111
- *Seattle:* 3240 Federal Building, 915 Second Ave., Seattle, WA 98174

K • The Securities and Exchange Commission

Like sheep, investors are prone to fleecing. This fact has been known for years, and the Securities and Exchange Commission (SEC) is one of the oldest of the federal regulatory agencies. Its basic purpose is to see that the sheep—er, investors—get a fair shake.

If you have a problem involving stocks, bonds, options, or misconduct on the part of a brokerage house or other securities organization, the SEC is one logical recourse. (Some other possible recourses are mentioned in the discussion of Securities in Part I of this book.) Based on the TARP study, I think the SEC does a reasonably good job of answering consumer complaints.

To send a complaint to SEC headquarters, write Director, Office of Consumer Affairs, Securities and Exchange Commission, 500 N. Capitol St., Washington DC 20549. Or you may prefer to contact the regional or branch office nearest you. The addresses of the fifteen SEC regional and branch offices, listed alphabetically by city, are below.

- *Arlington:* Ballston Center Tower 3, 4015 Wilson Blvd., Arlington, VA 22203
- *Atlanta:* Suite 788, 1375 Peachtree St. NE, Atlanta, GA 30309
- *Boston:* 150 Causeway St., Boston, MA 02114
- *Chicago:* Room 1204, Everett McKinley Dirksen Building, 219 S. Dearborn St., Chicago, IL 60604
- *Denver:* Room 640, Two Park Central, 1515 Arapahoe St., Denver, CO 80202
- *Detroit:* 1044 Federal Building, Detroit, MI 48226
- *Fort Worth:* 8th floor, 411 W. Seventh St., Fort Worth, TX 76102
- *Houston:* Room 5615, Federal Office and Courts Building, 515 Rusk Ave., Houston, TX 77002

- *Los Angeles:* Suite 1710, 10960 Wilshire Blvd., Los Angeles, CA 90024
- *Miami:* Suite 1114 DuPont Plaza Center, 300 Biscayne Boulevard Way, Miami, FL 33131
- *New York:* Room 1102, 26 Federal Plaza, New York, NY 10007
- *Philadelphia:* Room 2204 Federal Building, 600 Arch St., Philadelphia, PA 19106
- *Salt Lake City:* 3d floor, Federal Reserve Bank Building, 120 South State St., Salt Lake City, UT 84111
- *San Francisco:* 450 Golden Gate Ave., Box 36042, San Francisco, CA 94102
- *Seattle:* 3040 Federal Building, 915 Second Ave., Seattle, WA 98174

L • The Interstate Commerce Commission

The Interstate Commerce Commission (ICC) regulates buslines, the trucking industry, and to an extent the railroad industry. If you have a complaint in one of these areas, the ICC is often your chief potential source of help. (See also separate entries in Part I under Buses, Moving, and Trains.)

Many consumerists used to consider the ICC a classic example of an agency that was a captive of the commercial interests it was supposed to regulate. In the 1976 TARP study, it was one of the slowest of federal agencies in responding to consumer complaints, taking thirty-one days to answer the average one.

However, the ICC has lately shown some signs of being more responsive to consumer interests. One such sign has been the institution of toll-free telephone numbers to call with complaints. You can call the ICC's Washington headquarters toll-free by dialing 800-424-9312 or 800-424-9313. (From Florida, call 800-432-4537. From Washington DC itself, call 202-275-0860—not a toll-free number but a local call.) These numbers connect you to the ICC's National Complaint Center, which is ordinarily the place you should call with problems or complaints.

If you want to write the ICC, the headquarters address is Director, Consumer Assistance Office, Interstate Commerce Commission, Washington DC 20423.

The ICC also maintains regional offices in Atlanta, Boston, Chicago, Fort Worth, Philadelphia, and San Francisco. However, your first contact should normally be with the National Complaint Center in Washington DC.

M • The Civil Aeronautics Board

The Civil Aeronautics Board (CAB) handles complaints about, naturally enough, airlines. It handles them rather well, for the most part. The TARP study in 1976 found that the CAB answered the average complaint in about ten days. That's much quicker than most agencies managed. The CAB also got good grades in the study for the directness and clarity of its responses.

For an idea of your rights as an airline passenger, read the entry in Part I of this book on Airlines. If you feel your rights have been abridged, complain first to the airline and then, if you don't get satisfaction, to the Bureau of Consumer Protection, Civil Aeronautics Board, Washington, DC 20428.

N • How to Use Small Claims Court

Every ordinary citizen ought to be able to have his (her) day in court. That's part of the theory behind this country's judicial system, as it was originally conceived. But anyone who reads about two-year waiting periods for civil cases, or who knows about the stratospheric fees often charged by lawyers, quickly comes to understand that a lawsuit is not a practical way to solve most problems.

Small claims courts were designed to make justice reachable, tangible, and affordable—for ordinary people and for small cases. To some extent, these courts have done just that. As the name implies, small claims courts are designed to deal with legal disputes that do not involve much money. They have a dollar ceiling—usually $1,000, but it varies from state to state—and lawyers are not needed. They still fall short of the ideal for which they were conceived. Drop in at the average small claims court, and what you'll find, for the most part, is merchants winning judgments against delinquent consumers: The courts have become debt-collection devices. Worse yet, when a consumer goes to small claims court and wins, he or she may discover with intense annoyance that it's very difficult to collect on the judgment. You can wind up in the absurd position of having to go to court *again* to collect the money awarded you the first time. In the words of one writer on small claims courts, a victory amounts to a hunting license to try to collect the money awarded you.

Conceding these negatives, you should know that there are a lot of positive things to be said for small claims court. First, and perhaps foremost, ordinary consumers who file suits in small claims courts win about two-thirds of their cases. So, if you have a strong case, the odds are definitely in your favor. What's more, if you do win, the odds are that you'll collect. In short, though small claims courts in many parts of the country need reforming, they're still well worth using as they are.

How do you use small claims court? It's usually not difficult. First, call your county office building (or in large cities, city hall). Find out what the small claims court in your area is called, and where it's located. (If you have trouble getting this information, call the office of your state representative.

A staff member will probably try to help you.) Then call or stop by the court. The court clerk or other court personnel can usually guide you through the mechanics of filling out any necessary forms and arranging a court date.

Be sure to find out (1) any procedures you have to go through to serve your adversary with a summons; (2) whether your adversary's exact legal name and address must appear on the summons, and if so, where you most easily can find it; (3) whether you can sue your adversary in the small claims court nearest your home, or whether you must use the one closest to his place of business; and (4) whether your claim is within the court's dollar limit.

Do you need a lawyer? Emphatically not. Some jurisdictions actively discourage the use of lawyers, or even ban them. What's more, studies have shown that your chances of winning with a lawyer are no better than your chances without one.

The court session itself won't be intimidating. At the set time, you'll sit down in a room with your adversary and the judge. The judge will direct the proceedings in a brief and informal way. The rules of evidence, as practiced in trial courts, aren't strictly adhered to. The judge will ask you for your version of the dispute, and then ask your opponent for his version.

When you're in court, be forthright about your complaint and your claim. You don't need to apologize for asserting your rights. But don't be belligerent or wordy. Judges hear more speeches than they care to; they appreciate brevity.

Bring with you to court three copies of a one-page summary of your case, typewritten if possible. Give one to the judge, one to your opponent, and keep one for yourself. Such a summary can be extremely helpful in putting the issues in focus. It becomes especially important if the judge doesn't render his decision on the spot. He or she may hear testimony, then retire to make a decision in private. You may be notified of the decision by letter or postcard. In cases where there's a delayed decision, your summary may help remind the judge of the issues, in a framework that's advantageous to you.

If you win, wait a few days to see if your opponent forks over the money. Check to see how long he has to file an appeal. (In most cases, a plaintiff can't appeal a small claims court verdict, but a defendant can.) When the time for an appeal (often ten days or two weeks) has passed, phone or write your opponent and ask when you'll be paid.

If your opponent stalls, go back to court and ask for help in collecting. Often you'll have to fill out another form, and you end up back in court, where the judge orders your opponent to pay up or face penalties. If he still doesn't pay after that, he's liable to a contempt-of-court charge. You usually have to go to the county sheriff to enforce the contempt-of-court order. Naturally, you hope not to go through all this folderol. Perhaps 20 to 33 percent of small claims court judgments, nationwide, require extensive efforts to collect. Let's hope that yours isn't one of them.

In some cases, if you need help collecting, you have an option of going to the sheriff or the marshal. (No, we're not back in the Wild West; these offices still exist in many counties and cities.) Douglas Matthews, an expert on small claims courts, recommended in his book *Sue the B*st*rds* that you opt for the sheriff. That's because the marshal often operates by charging the debtor a fee, which is a percentage of the money collected. With a small claims court judgment, the amount at stake—and hence the fee—is small, so the collection effort may stay on the back burner. I once helped straighten out a case involving money awarded to a couple who'd purchased a defective refrigerator. The marshal's office had been "too busy" to help the couple collect—for over a year. The moral, I guess, is that small claims court, like many avenues of consumer recourse, can require assertiveness and persistence.

The cost of using small claims courts isn't high. It will usually cost you at most $15 to have your case heard, another $10 or so if you need help from the sheriff in collecting an award. In many cases, there are procedures under which your opponent may be required to reimburse you for these costs.

In terms of time, the procedure is more costly. You won't spend a lot of time in court, but you'll spend some time filling out forms and getting ready for your court hearing. If your opponent is recalcitrant, there may be delays and continuances. Since your time is valuable, you have to consider this factor in deciding whether to bring a small claims court action.

Consider, though—if it's any consolation—that your opponent may have to spend almost as much time on the proceeding as you do. In any case, small claims court is one forum he can't ignore, since he can be required by subpoena to show up. For this reason, it can be a very effective complaint resolution mechanism. If the money at stake or the principle at stake is important to you, and if you've tried simpler avenues without success, small claims court may be precisely what you need.

O • And Now, a Word from Your Lawyer

You may believe that involving a lawyer in settling a dispute is always a costly step. Well—not always. It may sound like gamesmanship to say so, but one important function a lawyer can serve is to intimidate your opponent. This may produce, for the first time, a genuine effort on your opponent's part to settle the dispute.

Here's one of my favorite examples, which involved a friend of mine, a young man. Soon to be married, he had a bathroom with a leaky roof and falling tiles. Requests to the landlord for service were met with the standard "we'll-look-into-it" response. The requests were escalated to complaints with no more results. Finally the young man turned to his uncle, a lawyer, for help. The uncle sent the landlord a letter on his firm's stationery. The letter was quite simple. It contained no assertions about the facts of the case, the condition of the bathroom, or the alleged irresponsibility of the landlord. All it said, in essence was, "I represent Mr. Kenneth Green, the occupant of apartment 2B in your building at 123 Main Street. I understand you are having a dispute with him over certain conditions in the apartment. I would appreciate your informing me, in writing, of your version of this dispute at your earliest convenience." That's all, just a simple request for the landlord's side of the dispute. The result: The landlord fixed up the bathroom immediately—several weeks, as it turned out, before the new bride moved in.

If you have a friend or relative who's a lawyer, you might understandably be reluctant to impose on him or her for legal advice. But you might feel comfortable asking the person to write a brief note, like the one described above. Even if you have to pay a lawyer, the cost of a cursory intervention like this should be minimal. And it may be all that's needed to wrap up the dispute.

P • If You Have to Go to Court

Small claims court is one thing. A full-scale lawsuit is another. There's no question about it: Litigation is costly and time-consuming. In a sense, this entire book is devoted to trying to help you solve problems without the need for a lawsuit. If you do find yourself in a lawsuit, what you need is quality legal advice—something I, a nonlawyer, couldn't possibly offer.

How do you find a good and affordable lawyer? One way is to seek out people who have had a legal problem similar to the one you're experiencing. Ask them who represented them, and how satisfied they were.

For straightforward legal problems, legal clinics may be an ideal source of legal advice. These are law firms that try to do a high-volume, comparatively low price business. They often specialize in handling such common problems as wills or uncontested divorces, and they often use nonlawyers to do much of the routine work. They may also rely on standard forms, in some cases, rather than drafting legal documents to order. If your case has few unusual twists, you may find that the smaller cost of a legal clinic more than makes up for the fact that you'll be receiving standardized, rather than custom-tailored legal advice. You can sometimes find legal clinics by watching ads in local newspapers, or by looking in the yellow pages of the phone book.

For further advice on selecting an attorney, I recommend the chapter "How to Choose a Lawyer," in *A Guide to Consumer Services* by the editors of Consumer Reports Books.

Before you consider the major effort and expense of a lawsuit, ask yourself how well you know and trust the attorney who's advising you. The more trust you have in your attorney, the more you'll be willing to let him (her) guide you in deciding whether a lawsuit is worth the cost involved. If you're dealing with a lawyer you know only slightly, keep in mind the possibility that the litigation could be more profitable for the lawyer than for you.

Discuss fees fully and candidly, in advance, with your attorney. In some cases, the attorney will serve for a contingent fee—a percentage of any future award you win. In that case, you'll pay nothing to the lawyer if you lose. But you should understand exactly how much of your award will go for legal expenses if you win.

It's often wise to disclose to your opponent that you're preparing a lawsuit. Most cases are settled out of court anyway. It's to the advantage of both parties to settle early, rather than late.

If and when the other side does make you a settlement offer, consider it carefully. That means get the offer in writing. Don't be rushed. Sit down and analyze the offer with the aid of your lawyer.

As a way of sharing legal costs, and being able to afford top-rank legal representation, consider the possibility of a class action suit. Such suits can be brought, under some circumstances, in either state or federal courts. However, there are substantial barriers to class action suits in the federal courts (erected by the Burger Supreme Court), and in many state courts as well. Your lawyer should be able to inform you of the situation in your state. If your case is appropriate for a class action suit, you may have the added satisfaction of bringing redress to many aggrieved consumers besides yourself.

Q • Your Friendly Local Consumer Group

Do you know the name of your local voluntary consumer organization? If not, join the crowd. Many people don't realize that there's a voluntary consumer group active in their area, perhaps because such group's bread-and-butter activities aren't always the stuff of which headlines are made. But such groups may be extremely helpful in mediating disputes and bringing moral pressure to bear on merchants or manufacturers to resolve complaints. Many such groups also work to prevent complaints, distribute marketplace information (e.g., buyers' guides to everything from local supermarket prices to the services of banks or physicians), and promote public-interest causes.

It's possible that by joining a local consumer group, you could make a contribution to your community and at the same time gain potential allies in disputes. Even if you don't join a group, you may still be able to get help from it.

If you already know the name and location of the voluntary consumer organizations active in your area, fine. If not, you can check with your local library, government officials, or media. Or look in the phone book under Consumer Association or Consumer Council of (wherever). If that fails, write to the Consumer Federation of America, 1012 14th St. NW, Washington DC 20005. It can usually tell you the identity of the nearest group or groups. There are more than two hundred scattered around the United States.

R • Ralph Nader and His Friends

Quite a few voluntary consumer groups are outcroppings of the Nader organization, and many of them reflect some of the passion and innovativeness of their (indirect) founder. Ralph Nader remains, in many ways, America's foremost consumer advocate. He no longer enjoys the uncritical, almost worshipful press coverage he commanded in the 1960s —and that's probably to the good. Years after he wrote *Unsafe at Any Speed* and battled General Motors about the safety of the Corvair, Nader has become an institution—and no institution should be invulnerable to criticism. The complaints against Nader now voiced by his critics are that he's spread himself too thin, and that he sometimes "shoots from the hip" without checking sufficiently for accuracy. Perhaps so. In my opinion, however, Nader has done, and continues to do, immense good.

On the national level, Nader's organizations include the

Center for the Study of Responsive Law (Nader's home base), Public Citizen (the fund-raising arm), Congress Watch (the political arm), the Corporate Accountability Research Group, the Aviation Consumer Action Project, and the Health Research Group. Other groups and projects have, or have at some point had, organizational or financial help from Nader.

On the state and local levels, the Nader organization has helped to launch voluntary groups that are usually called PIRGs. The acronym stands for Public Interest Research Group. There's a PIRG in most states, and there may be one near where you live. If you'd like to get involved with a PIRG or seek help from one with a problem, check first your local library, media, or telephone book. If you're still in doubt whether there's a PIRG near you, write the Center for the Study of Responsive Law, PO Box 19367, Washington, DC 20036.

S • Consumers Union

I really shouldn't mention Consumers Union in this book. The venerable nonprofit testing and consumer advocacy organization (publisher of *Consumer Reports*) doesn't actively encourage people to write to it with consumer complaints.

Also, anything I say about CU is biased, since I used to work there full-time and still do some free-lance work for the organization. I'm very fond of many people there.

But I'll mention CU anyway, because somehow its staffers do find time to help a fair number of individual consumers with complaints. There's no formal procedure for this, but the complaints sometimes find their way to a writer, engineer, or secretary who will take time out from other duties and go to bat for an individual consumer. In addition, complaints by consumers help CU decide what issues to tackle. CU's address is 256 Washington St., Mount Vernon, NY 10550.

Incidentally, if you read *Consumer Reports* regularly, you'll reduce your chances of being stuck in consumer-complaint situations in the future.

T • Action Lines

Newspapers, radio and TV stations often have action lines. You can write in (or, more rarely, phone in) and hope that the action line people will go to bat for you. When it works, it really works. Media people do have considerable clout. The implicit threat of unfavorable publicity is often enough to get a business to quit stalling and give a consumer what he or she deserves. Besides handling complaints, action lines can sometimes come up with answers for some pretty esoteric information requests.

Most action lines don't hesitate to broadcast or print their successes. But not many are forthright about their failures. And there are a lot of failures—mainly because there are a lot of complaints that action line people never have time to work on.

According to the TARP study, action lines typically receive anywhere from 400 to 14,000 complaints per month. That's testimony to their enormous visibility—and also to the high hopes consumers have for them. But some of those hopes get dashed, because most action lines don't have anywhere near sufficient staff to handle all the complaints received. Hiring volunteer help is sometimes forbidden, the TARP study said, by labor-management contracts at the newspapers or television stations.

So, unless your complaint is glamorous and exotic, or would make good copy, or happens to come at the right time of day, or happens to fall into the right place in someone's inbox, it may get lost. Many action lines, the TARP researchers reported, have sloppy bookkeeping (or none), hence no way to follow up and make sure that complaints get answered.

On the positive side, if your complaint does get attention, there's quite a good chance that the situation will be resolved to your satisfaction. It's something of a gamble. But then, you can't lose much by writing an action line—just time and stationery. Keep in mind that you can use out-of-town action lines for resolving disputes with out-of-town firms.

I recommend using action lines, but with certain guidelines in mind. I suggest you use them (1) for unusual complaints or information requests; or (2) in conjunction with other complaint-resolution methods; or (3) as a close-to-last resort. Think of it along the lines of buying a lottery ticket. It doesn't cost you much, the odds are against you, but the payoff can be quite handsome if you win.

U • The Power of the Media

Action lines aren't the only way you can harness the power of the media. Even more powerful, though even harder to get, is news coverage. If your complaint is unusual, if it has a bizarre or entertaining twist, or if you can show that a similar problem affects a lot of people in your community, you might be able to get radio, television, or newspaper reporters to throw a spotlight on your problem.

If you already know someone who works for one of the media, start with that person. If you don't, start writing letters. Write to the top editors or station managers, explaining why you think your complaint merits coverage. Write to reporters who have done stories on related topics in the past. Write to the consumer beat reporter, where there is one. And write letters to the editor, to be published in the "letters" or "opinion" section of your local paper.

A long shot? Yes, indeed. But if you succeed in getting

news coverage, it can be the sword that cuts the Gordian knot.

Incidentally, I see nothing wrong in trying to create a so-called media event to dramatize a problem. I recall one New York tenants' group that had some beefs with the landlord of their building. Among other things, they felt that the landlord was letting the building, which had been designed many years before by the renowned architect Sanford White, get a bit run down. As it happened, the landlord owned race horses. The group decided to picket, in horse and jockey costumes, outside a major New York race track. The group drafted a one-page press release and sent it to the media a couple of weeks in advance. Sure enough, when the costumed pickets started to pace outside the race track, television cameras were there.

V • Your Elected Representatives—They Work for You, Don't They?

A lot of people would never dream of asking for help from their city council representative, or mayor's office, or state representative or senator, or U.S. representative or senator. Why not? First, because people think that elected officials are too busy or too important (or, in some cases, too indifferent) to help them. Second, because—let's face it—many people couldn't name, say, their alderman, if you offered them $100 to do it.

I'll skip the lectures on how you should know who your elected representatives are. If you don't know, it's as simple as calling city hall, or the county building, or the League of Women Voters, or visiting your public library. Once you know, write or phone. Your elected representatives are elected to work for you. That's their job. That's why they're called public servants; they're supposed to serve you. And, though it may be a cliché, you do pay their salary.

Naturally, contacting your elected officials is a step to be taken only if you have a genuine grievance and other recourse avenues haven't brought you satisfaction. If you wrote your U.S. senator about your broken toaster before you wrote to the seller and manufacturer, you'd be a fool. But if you have a genuine problem and you've tried without success all the standard avenues, including the local and state consumer agencies and the Better Business Bureau, there's no reason why you shouldn't seek the aid of a politician. Particularly if your problem is with the government—social security, for example—your representative should be informed.

Politicians, like the media, have a lot of clout. One phone call or letter from a politician may sometimes produce a quick settlement of a dispute that's been dragging on for months.

Another reason why it can make sense to involve a politician in your problem is that you may not be the only one with the problem. If she or he sees a pattern in the problems brought in by constituents, a politician may be able to work toward broad-scale corrective measures, such as legislation.

W • Picketing

Picketing takes a bit of guts, but it can produce results. Consider, for example, the case of Jim Van Buskirk and the art course. Jim, who was living in San Francisco at the time, saw an advertisement for the course. A local artist of some note would teach the course, the ad said, and the classes would be small. Jim plunked his money down—scarce money, since Jim, though young, is disabled and can work only irregularly.

When the course began, he found that the classes were large, not small. The teacher wasn't the one named in the ad, and was inexperienced to boot. The chief attraction of the course for most of the students appeared to be the suggestive poses of the models.

Jim had nothing against other people's paying their money to see women model in suggestive poses. But that wasn't quite what he had in mind. "I just wanted to learn legitimate art," he said, "so I asked for a refund, covering all the classes but the two I had already attended." The people running the course refused to give the refund, saying they needed the full amount to cover rent on the building and other expenses. Jim called the San Francisco police, but they told him they had more important things on their minds. So "I went to Woolworth's, got me two pieces of posterboard and some paint, and made a sandwich sign. I walked up and down in front of the shop where the classes were held, carrying this sign that said these people were engaged in misrepresentation, and I wanted to warn the public. You'd be surprised how effective one person can be in front of a store, especially if he's disabled and has to carry a cane to walk. After about an hour and fifteen minutes they came out and gave me my refund—in cash."

Sometimes the threat of picketing is enough to produce action. Van Buskirk once rented a car from one of the major rental companies in the Chicago area. The rate was to be $14 a day, and no mileage charge. He entered the rental office at 5:45 P.M., left with the car at 6:15 P.M., and returned it at 7:00 P.M. the next day at a gas station that was licensed by the rental agency to accept returned vehicles. The charge came to an inexplicable $36, which Jim paid. Infuriated, he then went back to the rental office (taking a train and a bus to get there). "I can't afford to have you ripping me off," he told the manager. "I'm going to be out here picketing this weekend, and I'm going to bring my friends. What's more, I'm going to charge you three dollars an hour for my time, and the time of each person picketing your place, until you give me twenty dollars back on this bill."

The manager became extremely animated and began to raise his arms and his voice. "What do you want?" he asked, in seeming exasperation. (This, by the way, is a question every complaining consumer should always be glad to hear.)

"I want twenty-five dollars," Jim said.

"Wait a minute," said the manager, suddenly rational again. "A minute ago, you said twenty dollars."

"I decided I should add on the cost of my transportation here and back," Jim replied. The upshot: Jim got a $20 refund, and the manager personally drove him home. "It was," Jim recalls, "one of the quietest trips I've ever taken."

By the way, it should be noted that, even though Jim used unconventional methods to solve his problem, he used very conventional ones to lay the groundwork. He had saved a copy of the rental argeement, spelling out clearly what the charges were supposed to be. "The manager knew that I had proof that would stand up in court," he said.

X • Telling Daddy (The Uses of Parent Corporations)

Let's say you run your complaint up the corporate flagpole and no one salutes. In other words, the company's ignoring you. You may figure that your next recourse is a government agency or some other outside group. But that's not always so. A great many companies nowadays are subsidiaries of larger corporations. And the parent corporation may, in many instances, have a more liberal policy about satisfying complainants than does the subsidiary. In short, it's worth remembering your childhood ploy, "I'm going to tell Daddy on you."

How do you ascertain the identity of the parent company (if any) and its address? It's easy, given the resources of any decent public library. Among the best reference books to use for this purpose are the *Directory of Corporate Affiliations* and the *Standard Directory of Advertisers* (both published by National Register Publishing Co.), the *Trade Names Directory* (published by Gale Research), the *Standard & Poor's Registry of Corporations,* and the *Thomas Register of American Manufacturers.*

Then call or write the parent company, providing a brief description of your complaint and your request for a solution. You may be pleasantly surprised at the result.

Y • The Cops

Don't rule out the men (women) in blue as a source of help. Some police departments in large cities have antifraud units. Some police officials may know local avenues of recourse that you're unaware of. And if you think the person who took your money is about to skip town, it makes sense to call the police.

Z • How to Make a Stink (Effectively)

You've probably heard about the man who couldn't get satisfaction on his complaints about his new car. He finally painted it lemon yellow, and parked it in front of the dealer's with an appropriate sign.

You've heard, too, about people who mail strange and unsavory objects to politicians or corporate officials, in order to dramatize a grievance. And you've heard about services that will throw a pie in the face of your adversary, or deliver an insulting singing telegram.

All these tactics have their place, and you might even want to use one of them, or one equally bizarre, some time. But you don't have to cover your body with paint and parachute out of an airplane to make a point. There are quieter unconventional tactics that can be equally effective.

You remember Professor David Klein, whom I mentioned in the Introduction of this book. He employs a variety of unconventional tactics. One that he's used with good success lately he reserves for items under $15, not under warranty. "I simply send the damn thing back to the president of the company," he says. "And I send, not an angry letter, but one with a wry tone." Recently Professor Klein had trouble with a small kitchen appliance. He sent it to the president of the company with a covering letter. "Does your wife use one of these?" he asked. "Did you bother trying it out in a kitchen before manufacturing and selling it?" He got back a pleasant reply and a newer, better model.

An editorial writer at a newspaper where I used to work is a white-haired man, of gentle, dignified mien, in his early sixties. He illustrated how effective you can be with a complaint if you're willing to cause just a little bit of a scene. On the day in question, he'd bought a beef roast for dinner. When he got it home and unwrapped it, there was a lot of uncut fat —for which, of course, he'd paid a premium price. He and his wife decided to save the fat and cook the roast. When they did, a huge amount of additional fat drained off. The editor fished the package label, with weight and price indicated, out of the garbage can. He took the label and the remains of the cooked roast, plus the trimmed fat, to the store on a plate. Eyes turned. A crowd gathered. The editor patiently waited for service at the butcher's counter. When the butcher finally got to him, the editor gave a loud and lengthy explanation of why he felt the butcher had not given him his money's worth. He left the store with a full refund, plus a new roast, compliments of the house.

APPENDIX I

THE GRIPE INDEX: WHAT BOTHERS CONSUMERS MOST?

The Gripe Index is a measure of how common and serious a particular kind of consumer complaint is. The index is designed so that the highest (and worst) possible score is 100. Automobile repairs come near to achieving that score, with a 97. The score reflects both the geographical distribution and the severity of consumer complaints; scores are based on my 1975 survey of state consumer protection departments.*

Type of Complaint	*Gripe Index*
1. Automobile repairs	97
2. Automobile sales	83
3. Home improvements & repairs	65
4. Mail order	59
5. Mobile homes	43
6. Appliances & appliance repairs	34
7. Furniture & home furnishings	25
8. Credit	22
9. Landlord-tenant	21
10. Real estate	20

* A complaint that was the most common in a given state was given ten points; second most common, nine points, and so on, down to one. Scores were added for the 44 agencies that filled out this portion of my questionnaire. Thus the maximum raw score possible was 440. That would translate to a Gripe Index of 100. A raw score of 220 would translate to a Gripe Index of 50; a raw score of 110 would be an index of 25, and so on.

APPENDIX II

SCORECARD ON FEDERAL AGENCIES

An idea of how well the major federal consumer complaint handling agencies do their job can be gained from the TARP study, conducted by Technical Assistance Research Programs, Inc., under a contract from the U.S. Office of Consumer Affairs. The TARP study ran from 1975 to 1979, but the detailed data in this chart were from a 1975 phase of the study.

Agency	*% of Appropriate Responses*[1]	*% of Clear Responses*[2]	*Average Time for Response*
Federal Trade Commission	72%	93%	13 days
Food and Drug Administration	100%	97%	22 days
Consumer Product Safety Commission	93%	98%	19 days
Interstate Commerce Commission	93%	100%	31 days
Civil Aeronautics Board	97%	99%	10 days

[1] Responses were considered appropriate if they fit the complaint, whether the response was favorable or unfavorable.

[2] Responses were considered clear if the researchers judged them likely to be understood in light of the estimated sophistication and educational level of the complainant.

JOHN DORFMAN is the author of the syndicated consumer affairs column "Count Your Change," which appears in some 50 newspapers from Seattle to Washington, D.C. In 1970 he began writing for *The Home News,* a New Jersey daily; and two years later he went to the National Business News desk of The Associated Press. Before becoming a free-lance journalist, Dorfman served on the editorial staff of *Consumer Reports* magazine. He has contributed to *Money, Consumer Reports, Playboy,* and other magazines, and has written five books including *Consumer Survival Kit,* which was named one of the fifty best books of 1976 by *Library Journal.* He is a consultant to the New York State Consumer Protection Board and to Consumers Union.

The author was born in Chicago in 1947, and received his B.A. from Princeton and an M.F.A. from Columbia University. He lives in Evanston, Illinois, with his wife and two daughters.